D1266132

HISTORIC CHURCHES OF MISSISSIPPI

HISTORIC CHURCHES OF MISSISSIPPI

Sherry Pace

UNIVERSITY PRESS OF MISSISSIPPI   JACKSON

Essay and captions by

Richard J. Cawthon

A Mary Jayne G. Whittington Book in the Arts

www.upress.state.ms.us

The University Press of Mississippi is a member of the Association of American University Presses.

Manufactured in China

First edition 2007

Library of Congress Cataloging-in-Publication Data

Pace, Sherry.
Historic churches of Mississippi / Sherry Pace ; essay and captions by Richard J. Cawthon. — 1st ed.
p. cm.
Includes index.
ISBN-13: 978-1-57806-940-8 (cloth : alk. paper)
ISBN-10: 1-57806-940-8 (cloth : alk. paper)
1. Historic buildings—Mississippi—Pictorial works.
2. Church buildings—Mississippi—Pictorial works.
3. Church architecture—Mississippi—Pictorial works.
4. Cemeteries—Mississippi—Pictorial works.
5. Mississippi—History, Local—Pictorial works.
I. Cawthon, Richard J. II. Title.
F342.P325 2007
976.2—dc22 2006029066

British Library Cataloging-in-Publication Data available

Photographer's Preface

I was born in Jackson, Mississippi, and have lived in Madison County since 1983. I am a freelance outdoor photographer and am interested in a wide variety of subject matter that is featured on my Web site. Architectural photography has been a strong interest of mine for the past decade. Since the publication of my first book, *Victorian Houses of Mississippi*, by the University Press of Mississippi, my appreciation for architecture has continued to grow.

Many people have asked me how I first got started with photography. My husband is the one who discovered I had a talent in that field as he looked through our vacation shots taken nearly ten years ago. He encouraged me to pursue photography by participating in many exhibits, contests, and finally books. He is truly my hero for always being there for me and encouraging me to fulfill my dreams. He is my helpmate in the true sense of the word. I have also been asked many times where I received my photography training. I am self-taught and have learned to make my computer a darkroom by doing all my own editing of my digital photography work.

Whenever I traveled around the state, I was always drawn to the beautiful churches and would want to photograph them. I was intrigued by their diversity. Located in small towns, in cities, and on back roads, many were elaborate and others quaint. That's how I came up with the idea to do this second book. In fact, I had the idea for this church book from the very beginning, before my Victorian houses book. The whole state is represented well, with the churches being spread out all around Mississippi.

My purpose is to offer a photographic sampling, not an architectural digest, of these historic churches. They are presented in alphabetical order by city or town, with dates ranging from circa 1828 to circa 1928. It would have been impossible to include all the churches built during this one-hundred year span, but I have tried to provide an interesting variety, in well-known regions as well as in remote areas of our state.

The churches in the book were selected from files at the Historic Preservation Division of the Mississippi Department of Archives and History. Richard Cawthon, retired chief architectural historian for the Mississippi Department of Archives and History, wrote the informative captions and introductory essay explaining the various architectural styles and important historical facts, citing examples from my selection.

I do not have the words to truly express what making these two books has meant to me. I am acutely aware that I am helping preserve Mississippi's beautiful architectural heritage, especially that of the Mississippi Gulf Coast region, in a very special way. Hurricane Katrina made me even more aware of the importance of archiving history through photographs. I see the world through the eyes of a camera lens; life to me is a continuous collection of photographs. I hope you enjoy looking at these as much as I enjoyed taking them.

ACKNOWLEDGMENTS

I want first to thank God for allowing me to take and share the photographs in this book. Special thanks go, as always, to my wonderful husband, John, for, as he puts it, "driving Miss Sherry." With my very poor sense of direction, I would not have been able to make these books! Thanks to his navigational skills and overall knowledge of the state, that burden was lifted from me. I also want to thank our daughter, Hope, for her constant encouragement and belief in my work. I am grateful to everyone at the University Press of Mississippi for all their efforts with this project. Special thanks go to Richard Cawthon for the interesting captions and essays that he has written for both of my books.

Religious Architecture in Mississippi from the 1820s through the 1920s

Richard J. Cawthon

The religious architecture of Mississippi from the 1820s through the 1920s encompasses a variety of different styles and forms, ranging from simple wood-frame country churches to elaborate cathedrals, and including styles as diverse as Federal, Gothic Revival, Greek Revival, Italianate, Romanesque, Moorish, and Neoclassical Revival. This wide architectural variety is not as complex as it may initially appear, however, because most of the state's older churches can be broadly categorized as being either examples of a small range of traditional vernacular forms or expressions of one of two major stylistic themes—the Classical Tradition and the Neo-medieval Tradition.

The Classical Tradition embraces several architectural styles that are derived from the architecture of ancient Greece and Rome. These include the Federal and Greek Revival styles of the antebellum period, the Colonial Revival and the Neoclassical Revival that flourished in the early twentieth century, and the Georgian Revival that became increasingly popular in the 1930s and later. The Neo-medieval Tradition, inspired by the architecture of churches built during the Middle Ages, encompasses the Gothic Revival and the Romanesque Revival, in all of their variations, and, to some extent, the Tudor Revival as well.

Large, substantial churches built in larger towns from the 1820s through the 1920s can usually be classified into one or the other of these two traditions. Many smaller churches, particularly those located in smaller towns and rural areas, exhibit simplified vernacular interpretations of styles from these traditions, or combinations of two or more styles. There are also a few historic religious buildings that represent other architectural styles, such as the Moorish and Mission styles, that developed outside the mainstream of the Classical and Neo-medieval traditions. Not all of the state's older churches can be classified by style, however. Some older churches, particularly in rural areas, embody traditional vernacular building forms with only minimal expression of popular architectural styles.

TRADITIONAL VERNACULAR FORMS

The term "vernacular" refers to a customary way of doing things by persons who do not have formal academic training. The word is used by architectural historians in two different but closely related senses of meaning. In one sense of the word, it refers to buildings that exhibit traditional forms (recurring shapes and plans) that have been handed down from generation to generation by builders who have not had formal architectural education. This "traditional vernacular" approach to building is sometimes referred to as "folk" architecture.

In the other sense of the word, "vernacular" refers to the adoption or copying of aspects of more sophisticated architecture by local builders and craftsmen, without the direction of an architect, resulting in a simplified, less sophisticated, or less "correct" interpretation of an architectural style. In this sense, one can speak of a "vernacular Greek Revival" or "vernacular Gothic Revival" building.

Many of Mississippi's earliest churches exhibit a rather narrow range of recurring traditional vernacular forms. Of these, three main traditional forms were particularly important in the early and middle years of the nineteenth century.

The most common of these forms was a one-story building of simple rectangular shape, with a gabled roof and either one center door or two paired, symmetrically placed doors on the front gable end of the building. Examples with one center door include Hudsonville Presbyterian Church north of Holly Springs in Marshall County (1846) and China Grove Methodist Church[1] near Tylertown in Walthall County (1861). Examples of the same basic form but with paired front doors include Bethany Presbyterian Church near Centreville in Amite County (circa 1855) and Lebanon Presbyterian Church near Learned in Hinds County (1854 and later). It is believed that the widespread use of paired front doors was derived from a custom, in some churches, of having separate seating areas for men and for women. Not every church with twin entrances originally maintained gender-segregated seating, but some did, and twin doors became a customary element of the traditional building form which persisted long after the practice of separated seating died out.

A second traditional form is essentially a two-story version of the first form. These buildings customarily housed a fraternal lodge hall in the upper story and a church or school (or both) in the lower story. One of the few surviving active churches that exemplify this form is Shongalo Presbyterian Church in Vaiden (1874). Some older Masonic halls also retain this traditional vernacular building form.

A third important traditional form is a gable-roofed rectangular building that appears, on the exterior, as if it has two stories, but it actually contains a single large room, two stories in height, that serves as a preaching hall. The upper part of this room contains interior galleries or balconies that overlook the lower level and provide additional seating. The upper tier of windows provides light for this balcony area. A rare surviving example of this early building form is Washington United Methodist Church (1828) at Washington, northeast of Natchez, although alterations made in 1902 lowered its ceiling, changing it from its original interior configuration. A later and more elaborate example, interpreted in the Greek Revival style with a Classical portico and raised on a full-story basement, is Oakland Chapel at Alcorn State University (originally Oakland College) (1840–51). Its interior retains its original configuration.

THE CLASSICAL TRADITION DURING THE ANTEBELLUM PERIOD

The earliest of the architectural styles of the Classical Tradition to appear in Mississippi was the Federal style, which began to appear soon after 1800. This style is distinguished by the use of slender, attenuated Roman-inspired detailing and round or elliptical arched openings. Federal-style churches in Mississippi typically have a cupola, which is commonly octagonal in shape and capped by a small dome instead of a spire. The most distinctive surviving Federal-style church building in Mississippi is Rodney Presbyterian Church (1832) at Rodney in Jefferson County. Other church buildings with Federal-style features include Woodville United Methodist Church (1824) and St. Paul's Episcopal Church in Woodville (1824). First Presbyterian Church in Natchez was built in 1828–30 in the Federal style, but it was altered in the 1830s and 1850s, and some Greek Revival features were added. The design of Carmel Presbyterian Church, located southeast of Natchez in Adams County, is a scaled-down and simplified interpretation of the design of First Presbyterian Church in Natchez, including its Federal-style cupola. The detailing of Carmel Church, however, displays characteristics of the Greek Revival style.

From the late 1830s until the Civil War, the Greek Revival was the dominant architectural style in Mississippi. Inspired by the architecture of temples built by the ancient Greeks, it was characterized by broad proportions, shallow pitched roofs, columns and entablatures in the Greek architectural orders, and rectangular openings instead of the round and elliptical arches of the Federal style. One of the first notable works of Greek Revival religious architecture in the state was the remodeling of Trinity Episcopal Church in Natchez. Originally built in 1822 in the Federal style, it was substantially remodeled in 1838, and was given a Greek Revival portico. Other notable surviving Greek Revival churches are Oakland Chapel at Alcorn State University (1840–51), College Hill Presbyterian Church north of Oxford (1846), Kingston United Methodist Church in the Kingston community southeast of Natchez (1856–57), Zion Chapel African Methodist Episcopal Church (originally Second Presbyterian Church) in Natchez (1858), and Provine Chapel at Mississippi College in Clinton (1859). Simpler vernacular Greek Revival churches include Carmel Presbyterian Church southeast of Natchez (previously mentioned in regard to its Federal-style cupola) and Liberty Presbyterian Church (circa 1850). Mississippi lost one of its most attractive vernacular Greek Revival churches in 2003, when Bethel Presbyterian Church near Columbus in Lowndes County, dating from 1844–45, was destroyed by a tornado.

By the time Mississippi began to rebuild in the aftermath of the Civil War, the Greek Revival style had fallen out of fashion, but a few modest vernacular churches with Greek Revival characteristics were built after the war, such as Vaiden United Methodist Church (1871). One of the few classically inspired churches built in Mississippi during the 1870s was Jefferson Street United Methodist Church in

Natchez (1870–76), which has both Italianate and Romanesque features. By the 1870s, the Neo-medieval styles had become so popular that no other substantial churches in the Classical Tradition were to be built in the state for nearly thirty years. The Classical Tradition would not return to the religious architecture of Mississippi until after 1900.

THE GOTHIC REVIVAL FROM THE 1830S THROUGH THE 1870S

During the Victorian era, extending from the 1830s through the end of the nineteenth century, there was a great popular fascination with the Middle Ages, both in England and in the United States. In architecture, this fascination was expressed by the development of two related architectural styles, the Gothic Revival and the Romanesque Revival, both based upon the architecture of the Middle Ages. The first of these styles to arise was the Gothic Revival. It had first appeared in the late eighteenth century as a sort of picturesque novelty, a superficial application of medieval-inspired features for an antiquarian visual effect, but gradually the architecture of the Middle Ages came to be studied, copied, and adopted more seriously, and the Gothic Revival emerged as a style of architecture. The Gothic Revival developed into a very significant movement in religious architecture in England in the 1830s under the influence of the Ecclesiological movement, which was an effort to revive within the Church of England a more formal and ceremonial "high church" or "Anglo-Catholic" style of worship. Architectural theorists of the Ecclesiological movement believed that the "Gothic" architecture of the Middle Ages was the most appropriate setting for this more formal manner of worship, and they urged the building of new churches that reflected the architectural qualities of late medieval English churches. Among the features that distinguished these Gothic churches were relatively dark interiors, intended to convey a sense of mystery and to draw attention to the prominent altar; stained glass windows; steeply pitched or vaulted ceilings; and the characteristic use of pointed arches throughout the design, particularly evident on doors and windows. In the United States, the Ecclesiological movement began to have a strong influence in the Episcopal Church in the 1840s, and by the end of that decade the Gothic Revival had become the favored style for new churches built for Episcopal congregations and for many Catholic parishes as well.

The Gothic Revival appeared in Mississippi surprisingly early. Churches with some Gothic detailing were built as early as the late 1830s. The oldest example of Gothic Revival religious architecture in Mississippi is a private chapel near Natchez that was built about 1837. Another of the earliest churches in the state to be designed with a distinct Gothic character, on its exterior at least, was Christ Church in Vicksburg, built from 1839 to 1841. The first church in Mississippi to fully embody the design principles of the Ecclesiological movement was the Chapel of the Cross in Madison County, which was begun about 1849–50 and consecrated in 1852. During the 1850s numerous Gothic Revival churches of brick construction were built throughout Mississippi for Episcopal congregations, including St. John's in Aberdeen (1853), Christ Church at Church Hill (1857–58), St. Peter's in Oxford (1857–58), Christ Church in Holly Springs (1858), and St. Paul's in Columbus (1859). Several substantial Catholic churches were also built in the Gothic Revival style during the 1840s and 1850s, including

St. Mary's Cathedral (now called St. Mary Basilica) in Natchez (1842–59) and St. Joseph's in Port Gibson (1850–51). Another notable Gothic Revival church from this period was (Old) St. Paul's Catholic Church in Vicksburg, which had been built about 1850 but was destroyed by the tornado that ravaged downtown Vicksburg in 1953.[2]

The proponents of Gothic Revival religious architecture during the 1840s and 1850s considered it to be best suited for construction in stone or brick, but the style was also adapted to wood-frame construction by such prominent architects of the Ecclesiological movement as Richard Upjohn and Frank Wills, who realized that many smaller, newer, and less prosperous congregations would find it necessary to build in wood. Grace Episcopal Church in Canton (1853) and the Church of the Good Shepherd in Terry (1860) are antebellum examples of this variation of the Gothic Revival style, sometimes called "Carpenter Gothic" architecture.

Because of the popularity of the Gothic Revival style, in secular as well as religious architecture, it was not uncommon, in the 1840s and 1850s, for Gothic decorative elements—pointed windows in particular—to be used in the design of buildings that were not otherwise Gothic in character, as can be seen at (Old) St. Joseph's Catholic Church (now called the Church of the Yellow Fever Martyrs) in Holly Springs (circa 1842), Fredonia United Methodist Church near Como in Panola County (1848), Mt. Zion Missionary Baptist Church in Rodney (circa 1850), and St. Mark's Episcopal Church in Raymond (1854).

Due to the social and economic disruption brought about by the Civil War and Reconstruction, very few substantial brick Gothic Revival churches were built in Mississippi during the 1860s and 1870s. The Catholic Church of the Assumption in Columbus was begun during the Civil War, in 1863, but construction was interrupted by the war and the building was not completed until 1878. A relatively modest Gothic Revival church of brick construction built during the postwar period was St. Clement's Episcopal Church in Vaiden, which was erected in 1876. Generally, however, the construction of substantial Gothic churches of brick or stone did not resume until the 1880s. In the immediate postwar era, the building of less expensive wooden churches was much more widespread. Among the more notable Carpenter Gothic churches built during this period were Sacred Heart Catholic Church at Rodney (1867–68) (now located at Grand Gulf Military Park near Port Gibson), Holy Innocents Episcopal Church in Como (1872), the Episcopal Church of Our Savior in Iuka (1873), the Episcopal Church of the Redeemer in Biloxi (1873–74), and Wesson Presbyterian Church (1877–78). More modest examples include St. Joseph Catholic Church in Woodville (1873), St. Mary's Episcopal Church at Enterprise (1874), and the Episcopal Church of Our Redeemer in Magnolia (circa 1875).

THE ROMANESQUE REVIVAL FROM THE 1850S THROUGH THE 1880S

Despite the popularity of the Gothic Revival style during the 1840s and 1850s, its strong association with the Ecclesiological movement caused it to be considered by some religious leaders and architectural writers, at that time, to be inappropriate for churches that did not embrace a formal liturgical approach to worship. By the mid-1850s, the Romanesque Revival style was being promoted by architectural writers as an alternative to the Gothic

Revival, better suited, they believed, for churches with a less liturgical manner of worship. In theory, the Romanesque Revival was based on the round-arched architecture of England during the Norman period, before the Gothic style became widespread, but the Romanesque Revival was also an American interpretation of the contemporary German "Rundbogenstil" ("round-arch style"), which was a flexible style, loosely based on European medieval models, that influenced both Romanesque Revival and Italianate architecture in the United States from the 1850s through the 1870s. Whatever its exact origins, the Romanesque Revival style became popular in the late 1850s, particularly for Presbyterian and Methodist churches. In Mississippi, two notable Romanesque Revival churches were completed shortly before the Civil War, both in the town of Port Gibson—First Presbyterian Church (1859) and Port Gibson United Methodist Church (1858–60). Two other important surviving Romanesque Revival churches were begun just before the Civil War but completed later. First United Methodist Church in Columbus was begun in 1860, but construction was interrupted by the Civil War, and it was completed in 1866. First Presbyterian Church in Holly Springs was begun in 1860, and its construction, too, was interrupted by the Civil War. It was completed in 1869. The ornate Church of the Holy Trinity (Episcopal) in Vicksburg was begun in 1870 and completed in 1880. Another significant Romanesque Revival church, First Presbyterian Church in Oxford, was built in 1880. The popularity of Romanesque Revival religious architecture declined in Mississippi during the 1880s, but it revived in the 1890s with the introduction of the auditorium-plan church.

THE GOTHIC REVIVAL FROM THE 1880S THROUGH THE EARLY 1900S

By the 1880s Mississippi's economy was recovering from the destruction and turmoil of the Civil War, in large part due to a boom in the lumber industry and improved transportation provided by an expanding network of railroads. The 1880s and 1890s saw widespread construction of substantial brick churches throughout the state. By this time, the popularity of the Gothic style had caused it to lose its strongly liturgical connotation, and it was becoming much more widely accepted by denominations other than the Episcopal and Catholic churches. This was, in part, because the style had diverged into two different modes or degrees of formality, which can be referred to as "High Gothic" and "Low Gothic." High Gothic religious architecture continued to emulate the Gothic churches of the Middle Ages, and continued to be favored by many Episcopal and Catholic congregations. High Gothic churches built in Mississippi from the 1880s into the first decade of the twentieth century included St. Patrick's Catholic Church in Meridian (1886), All Saints Episcopal Church in Grenada (1889–90), the Catholic Church (later Cathedral) of St. Peter the Apostle in Jackson (1897–1900), the Catholic Church (later Cathedral) of the Nativity of the Blessed Virgin Mary in Biloxi (1901–2), St. Andrew's Episcopal Church (later Cathedral) in Jackson (1903), and St. Joseph's Catholic Church in Greenville (1908). Less ornate examples (which could be said to occupy a middle position between High and Low Gothic) include St. Paul's Episcopal Church in Meridian (1902), the Church of the Nativity (Episcopal) in Macon (1907–8), Grace Episcopal Church in Okolona (1908), Trinity Episcopal Church in Hattiesburg (1912), and the Episcopal Church of the Resurrection in Starkville (1913). The Episcopal churches in Okolona and Starkville were both patterned after the old St. Columb's Chapel in Jackson (no longer extant), which was the chapel of the bishop of the Episcopal Diocese of Mississippi from 1894 to 1902.

"Low Gothic" architecture simplified the medieval-inspired details and incorporated them into broader, more open, less ornate buildings that functioned more as preaching halls than as ceremonial spaces. By the late 1880s, Low Gothic religious architecture came to be widely accepted for Methodist, Presbyterian, and Baptist churches. Examples include (Old) First Baptist Church in West Point (1888) (no longer extant), the old sanctuary (1889) of First Baptist Church in Starkville, Carrollton Baptist Church in Carrollton (1894), the (Old) First Methodist Church in West Point (later First Christian Church, from 1920) (1895), First Presbyterian Church in Aberdeen (1895–96), and First United Methodist Church in Lexington (1897). Some of these churches applied High Gothic exterior features, such as stepped buttresses and tall spires, to buildings that were otherwise Low Gothic in character, with wide plans, broad windows, and elevated rostrums instead of recessed chancels. Stylistic description is complicated somewhat by the use of the term "High Victorian Gothic" to describe the particularly elaborate detailing applied to some Late Victorian churches, such as the bands of brick in a contrasting color seen on Main Street Presbyterian Church in Columbus (1885).

Some churches from this period have an "Eclectic Gothic" character, combining Gothic features with elements derived from other sources, such as the Queen Anne style, Stick style, or Shingle style. Among the more notable Eclectic Gothic churches from the 1880s into the 1910s are Grace Episcopal Church in Carrollton (1883), St. James Episcopal Church in Port Gibson (1884–85; enlarged circa 1897), St. John's Episcopal Church in Ocean Springs (1892), the Episcopal Church of the Nativity in Greenwood (1902), St. George's Episcopal Church in Clarksdale (1904), and Immanuel Episcopal Church in Winona (1909–10). Two important examples that no longer survive were (Old) St. James Episcopal Church in Greenville (1884, enlarged in 1895) and the second building of the Church of the Redeemer in Biloxi (1891), both of which exhibited a combination of Gothic Revival and Shingle-style features.

Many African American churches were newly organized in the decade following the end of the Civil War. As they acquired the financial means to do so, numerous African American congregations located in larger towns undertook the construction of substantial church buildings. From the 1880s through the 1910s these congregations generally favored the prevailing Gothic Revival style. Notable surviving examples include Holy Family Catholic Church in Natchez (1894), Jackson Street Missionary Baptist Church in Vicksburg (1905), Asia Baptist Church in Lexington (1908), and Rose Hill Baptist Church in Natchez (1908).

Carpenter Gothic architecture (the expression of the Gothic Revival style in wood construction) had enormous popularity in Mississippi between about 1880 and about 1910, a period corresponding with the great lumber boom. Among the many Carpenter Gothic churches that survive from this period are Magnolia Presbyterian Church (1881–82), Bogue Chitto United Methodist Church (1883), St. Francis of Assisi Catholic Church in Brookhaven (1888), Handsboro Presbyterian Church in Gulfport (1891), Shubuta United Methodist Church (1891), St. John the Baptist Catholic Church in Sardis (1891), Shubuta Baptist

Church (1894), Main Street United Methodist Church in Bay St. Louis (1895), Carrollton Presbyterian Church (1897), St. Mary Episcopal Church in Lexington (1900), Berwick Baptist Church near Liberty (1901), Pocahontas United Methodist Church (1902), Vernal Presbyterian Church near Leakesville (1906–8), and Woodville Presbyterian Church (circa 1909). The former Episcopal Church of the Epiphany (1887), which was originally located at Hermanville in Claiborne County, was moved to Jackson in the 1980s and is now the chapel at the Mississippi Agriculture and Forestry Museum.

NEO-MEDIEVAL AUDITORIUM-PLAN CHURCHES OF THE 1890S THROUGH THE EARLY 1920S

The 1880s saw the introduction of a new architectural form for American churches. Combining an exterior appearance derived from traditional religious architecture with an internal configuration derived from the architecture of theaters, this new form, called the "auditorium church" or "auditorium-plan church," was designed to provide an optimal setting for preaching. The auditorium-plan church is distinguished by a worship space that consists of a wide auditorium with a floor that slopes downward toward a raised pulpit platform, and a radial configuration of seating set in concentric curving arcs. In most cases the seating is in the form of curved pews, but in a few rare cases curved rows of individual folding theater seats are used (as at First Presbyterian Church in Yazoo City). In many cases the main axis of this curved seating is set on a diagonal to the main axis of the building, though in other cases the seating is arranged on the main center axis.

About the same time that the auditorium-plan church was beginning to become popular, a new approach to providing religious education in Sunday schools, called the "Akron Plan," was being promoted. Akron Plan Sunday schools utilized a central lecture hall surrounded by an array of small classrooms that opened into it but which could be closed off, by sliding or folding partitions, for small-group studies tailored to various age groups. Facilities for Akron Plan Sunday schools were often incorporated into the designs of auditorium-plan churches, typically in a manner that allowed the Sunday school lecture hall to open up into the auditorium-sanctuary by the moving aside of a partition, allowing the Sunday school lecture hall to serve as overflow seating space for the sanctuary. Churches that contained this combination of facilities were sometimes referred to, loosely, as "Akron Plan churches," and the term has sometimes been inaccurately applied to auditorium-plan churches generally, even if they never accommodated the Akron Plan Sunday school system.

From the late 1880s through the early decades of the twentieth century the auditorium-plan church enjoyed great popularity in Mississippi, and many buildings of this type were built throughout the state, particularly for Baptist, Methodist, and Presbyterian congregations. During the 1890s and early 1900s, auditorium-plan churches were typically designed in either the Gothic Revival or Romanesque Revival style. Some Neo-medieval auditorium churches continued to be built through the 1910s and into the early 1920s, though during this period Neoclassical designs became increasingly popular. Many of the finest auditorium-plan churches in Mississippi (and indeed throughout the South) were designed by Reuben Harrison Hunt of Chattanooga, Tennessee. During the 1890s and early 1900s many of Hunt's auditorium churches were designed in the Romanesque Revival style, including (Old) First Baptist Church in Meridian (1892–93) (no longer extant), First United Methodist Church in Greenwood (1898), Moore Memorial United Methodist Church in Winona (1898), First Presbyterian Church in Vicksburg (1906–8), Bay Street Presbyterian Church in Hattiesburg (1907–8), and First United Methodist Church in Pontotoc (1910). Other notable Romanesque auditorium-plan churches are (Old) First Presbyterian Church (now the Mary Ricks Thornton Cultural Center) in Kosciusko (1899), First Christian Church in Water Valley (circa 1905), and Bethel African Methodist Episcopal Church in Vicksburg (1912).

Auditorium-plan churches in the Gothic Revival style designed by R. H. Hunt included First Baptist Church in Columbus (1908) and First United Methodist Church in Aberdeen (1912). Other surviving Gothic Revival auditorium churches in Mississippi are First Presbyterian Church in Grenada (1905), Cleveland Street Associate Reformed Presbyterian Church in New Albany (1905), First Presbyterian Church in Yazoo City (1905–6), First Presbyterian Church in Brookhaven (1906–7), First United Methodist Church in Yazoo City (1907), First Baptist Church in Macon (1909), Main Street United Methodist Church in Hattiesburg (1907–10), First Presbyterian Church in Meridian (1912), and J. J. White Memorial Presbyterian Church in McComb (1921).

THE GOTHIC REVIVAL IN THE 1910S AND 1920S

In the closing years of the nineteenth century, several prominent American architects and architectural theorists, most notably Ralph Adams Cram of Boston, became concerned that Gothic Revival architecture in the United States during the Late Victorian period had strayed too far from its historic roots and had lost its spiritual qualities. Cram advocated a more refined, more intellectual approach to Gothic religious architecture. Architectural historians have struggled with a name for this "new" approach, which has sometimes been called the "Late Gothic Revival" or "Neo-Gothic," though neither of these terms seems quite accurate. In the early years of the twentieth century, this revitalized Gothic style was particularly favored by Episcopalians and Catholics, but it became increasingly popular with other denominations through the 1910s and 1920s.

Mississippi saw a resurgence of interest in the Gothic Revival from the mid-1920s into the 1930s. The state's most elegant expression of Gothic architecture from this period is First Presbyterian Church (later First-Trinity Presbyterian Church) in Laurel (1924–25), designed by Rathbone DeBuys of New Orleans with interior design by the firm of Watson and Boaler of Chicago. Other examples include Crawford Street United Methodist Church in Vicksburg (1925), First Presbyterian Church of Greenwood (1925–26), First Baptist Church in Jackson (1924–27, later enlarged and remodeled), First United Methodist Church in Booneville (1928), and First United Methodist Church in New Albany (1928). Many Gothic Revival churches from the 1920s and later show the influence of architecture of the Tudor era, which came to be favorably regarded by many Episcopalians, Presbyterians, and Methodists because of its historical association with the beginnings of the Reformation in England. The Gothic Revival churches built for Presbyterian, Methodist, and Baptist congregations in the 1920s tended to have a greater degree of formality to their plans than in the previous three decades. The auditorium plan was declining in popularity by this time, and most of these churches were arranged with a more rectilinear placement of pews on either side of a center aisle. This greater formality was typically expressed on the exterior by an entrance portal placed in the center of the façade, instead of the corner entrances that were more typical of auditorium-plan churches. This approach to Gothic Revival religious architecture continued into the 1930s and later.

THE ROMANESQUE REVIVAL IN THE 1910S AND 1920S

Many of the finest Catholic and Episcopal churches built in Mississippi during the 1910s and 1920s, as well as one of the most interesting Methodist churches of that time, were designed in a refined and historically based approach to the Romanesque style, drawing inspiration particularly from the medieval Romanesque churches of Italy. Churches showing this more historical approach to Romanesque architecture include St. John's Episcopal Church in Laurel (1914), First United Methodist Church in Clarksdale (1917), St. Alphonsus Catholic Church in McComb (1922), the Chapel of St. Augustine's Seminary in Bay St. Louis (circa 1926), Sacred Heart Catholic Church in Canton (1928), St. Mary's Episcopal Church in Vicksburg (1928), and the Church of the Immaculate Conception in Laurel (1929).

THE MOORISH STYLE

Much of the popularity of the Gothic Revival, especially during the nineteenth century, was due to the perception that it was a distinctly Christian form of architecture that was especially appropriate for the design of churches. Because of this perception, the Gothic style, despite its great popularity, was regarded with understandable hesitancy by Jewish congregations, although some Gothic Revival synagogues were built, such as the temple (no longer extant) that was built on South State Street in Jackson for the Beth Israel congregation in 1874.[3] Many Jewish congregations sought to find an architectural expression that seemed appropriately sacred without being particularly identified with Christianity. During the 1880s and 1890s, many synagogues in the United States were built in a style that was evocative of the period of Moorish dominion in Spain, where a vibrant Jewish culture had flourished. The oldest surviving synagogue building in Mississippi, Temple Gemiluth Chassed in Port Gibson (1891), is a particularly distinctive example of this Moorish-inspired architecture. A more modest example is Temple B'nai Sholom in Brookhaven (1896), where a subtle Moorish character is conveyed by the shapes of the windows and the panels in the upper part of the tower.

THE RETURN OF THE CLASSICAL TRADITION AFTER 1900

By the late 1890s, two approaches to the revival of classically inspired design had begun to appear in secular architecture in the United States. These were the Colonial Revival, which drew inspiration from the architecture of the colonial period on the Eastern Seaboard, and "Beaux Arts Classicism," an ornate but carefully disciplined approach to Classical Revival architecture.

During the first decade of the twentieth century, the Colonial Revival had a considerable influence on secular architecture in Mississippi, especially in the design of residences, but its influence on religious architecture at the time was minimal. One of the few examples of Colonial Revival religious architecture in the state during that period was the rebuilding of Pine Ridge Presbyterian Church near Natchez in 1909, to replace a church built in 1828 that had been destroyed by a tornado in 1908. With its simple gable-roofed form and round-arched windows, it is somewhat evocative of the small brick churches of the colonial era in Virginia and the Carolinas.

Of much greater impact on the religious architecture of Mississippi in the early decades of the twentieth century was the introduction of Beaux Arts Classicism, which appears to have first arrived with the construction of the Ricks Memorial Library in Yazoo City, begun in 1900 and completed in 1902. Much more widely known, however, and much more influential, was the construction of the "New" Mississippi State Capitol, which was begun in 1901 and completed in 1903. The New Capitol was the first large public building in Mississippi designed according to the precepts of Beaux Arts Classicism, a formal and highly sophisticated style of Classical Revival architecture that had been introduced from France and was being practiced by architects who had studied at the École des Beaux-Arts (the School of Fine Arts) in Paris. This approach to architecture used a highly structured plan and a careful relationship of Classical components to produce ornate and monumental buildings. Although some architectural historians treat Beaux Arts Classicism as a style unto itself, in contrast to a more austere but contemporaneous style labeled "Neoclassical Revival," these two approaches to Classical architecture are perhaps more clearly understood as two aspects or polarities of the same movement, which can broadly be called the Neoclassical Revival. This way of perceiving the Classical Revival architecture of the early twentieth century is much more applicable to the character of the many Classical Revival public buildings, churches, and private residences that were built throughout Mississippi from the early 1900s into the 1930s. Most of these buildings were neither ornate Beaux Arts compositions nor austere Neoclassical designs, but could more accurately be described as fitting somewhere between the two. In any case, the more ornate Beaux Arts Classicism was the first mode of "High Classicism" to arrive in Mississippi, appearing in both the Ricks Library and the New Capitol.

Almost immediately following the completion of the New Capitol, public and institutional buildings in the Neoclassical Revival style—courthouses, city halls, schools, collegiate buildings, and banks—began to appear in communities throughout the state. As a result, the Romanesque Revival fell out of fashion for public buildings seemingly overnight. It took somewhat longer for the Neoclassical Revival to become popular for religious architecture. Indeed, the Gothic Revival and Romanesque Revival never actually fell out of fashion for religious buildings but continued alongside the Neoclassical Revival during the 1910s and saw a resurgence in the 1920s.

The first religious building in Mississippi designed in the new Classical Revival style was apparently Temple B'nai Israel, the Jewish synagogue in Natchez, begun in 1904 and completed in 1905. It is an ornate work of Beaux Arts architecture designed by H. A. Overbeck of Dallas, Texas. An almost identical building, Hebrew Union Temple in Greenville, also designed by Overbeck, was built in 1906. The same year saw the completion of another Beaux Arts synagogue, the (Old) Temple Beth Israel (no longer extant) in Meridian. A smaller, wood-frame synagogue with Classical Revival features, Temple Beth El in Lexington, was built in 1905.

The first Christian house of worship built in the new Classical Revival style may have been the (Old)

First Baptist Church (no longer extant) in Greenwood, which was begun about 1908 and dedicated in 1910. It was an ornate Beaux Arts building with a tetrastyle (four-column) portico and a large dome. After having been replaced by a new sanctuary in 1976, it was demolished about 1985.[4] Another Neoclassical Revival church built at about the same time was Central Baptist Church in Newton (1908–10), which later became the Newton City Hall.

During the 1910s and 1920s many elegant, dignified Neoclassical Revival churches were built throughout Mississippi, mostly for Baptist, Methodist, and Presbyterian congregations. These churches were characteristically auditorium-plan buildings with radial seating, some of which had interiors arranged on a diagonal axis, while others were arranged on a center axis. Among the more notable surviving examples are Como United Methodist Church in Como (1912), First United Methodist Church in Gulfport (1912–13), First Presbyterian Church in Winona (1913), Galloway Memorial United Methodist Church in Jackson (1913–15), Dantzler Memorial United Methodist Church in Moss Point (1914), First United Methodist Church in Brookhaven (1916–17), First United Methodist Church in Cleveland (1917), First Baptist Church in Canton (1918), Clarksdale Baptist Church (1919–20), Lyon Baptist Church near Clarksdale (circa 1920–25), Central United Methodist Church in Columbus (1921), First United Methodist Church in Canton (1922), First Baptist Church in Leland (1922–23), the old sanctuary of First Baptist Church in Clinton (1923), Ahavath Rayim Synagogue in Greenwood (1923), First Baptist Church in Holly Springs (1923), First Baptist Church in New Albany (1923–25), First Presbyterian Church in Starkville (1924–26), First United Methodist Church in Starkville (1925), First Baptist Church in Hazlehurst (1926), and First United Methodist Church in Belzoni (1927). Neoclassical Revival religious architecture declined in popularity in the late 1920s and very few examples were built after 1929, by which time a resurgence of interest in the Gothic style had occurred, while the Classical tradition shifted toward the Georgian Revival, which grew in importance in the 1930s and beyond.

THE SPANISH COLONIAL AND MISSION STYLES

As the Colonial Revival and the Georgian Revival drew inspiration from the architecture of the colonial era of the English-settled area of the East Coast, a parallel movement was inspired by the architecture of the Spanish Colonial period in California and Texas. It was particularly popular in the southwestern states and in Florida, but Mississippi was receptive to it as well. The more elaborate version of this architecture is referred to as Spanish Colonial Revival, while a simpler, more abstract version is called the Mission style. Although these styles were most popular for residential and institutional architecture, several notable Spanish-inspired churches were built in Mississippi during the 1920s, of which the finest was (Old) St. John the Evangelist Catholic Church in Gulfport (1923–24) (no longer extant). Leland United Methodist Church (1923–24) is a notable example of the simpler Mission style.

OTHER STYLES AND INFLUENCES

The styles of the Classical Tradition and the Neomedieval Tradition, along with the Moorish and Spanish-inspired styles and the major traditional vernacular forms, provide contexts for understanding most of the architecturally notable churches and synagogues of Mississippi from the 1820s through the 1920s, but there are some religious buildings that do not fit neatly into those stylistic themes. Some have features of the Victorian Queen Anne style; others show the influence of the Arts and Crafts movement of the early 1900s. Some churches exhibit combinations of stylistic influences, and others are best understood as expressions of the creativity of individual architects or builders.

One of the most distinctive of the historic churches of Mississippi is First Presbyterian Church in Pontotoc. Built in 1915, it is notable for its unusual Prairie Style character. Its design, with its crisp geometrical composition and sparse decorative detailing derived from the structural form itself, was quite avant-garde for its time and anticipated architectural developments that would shape the religious architecture of the state later in the twentieth century.

Each of the buildings depicted in this book, from modest Federal-style churches of the 1820s to ornate Neoclassical auditorium-plan churches of the 1920s, from the medieval-inspired Gothic Revival to the forward-looking Prairie Style, has an important place in the rich and diverse architectural heritage of Mississippi. Moreover, these historic churches and synagogues provide enduring physical testimony to the importance of religion in the lives of Mississippians for the past two centuries. Mississippi's historic religious architecture is a profoundly meaningful cultural patrimony that deserves to be recognized, respected, and preserved as a legacy for future generations.

NOTES

1. This congregation is no longer active. Most of the older Methodist churches of Mississippi were originally organized as congregations of the Methodist Episcopal Church, South. After several reorganizations, the national body with which most of these Methodist Churches are affiliated is now called the United Methodist Church, and its congregations use this name as well. For the sake of consistency with current names, Methodist churches in Mississippi that have active congregations are referred to in this book with the words "United Methodist Church" in their names.

2. Information about Old St. Paul's Catholic Church in Vicksburg and a photograph of the building are included in Mary Carol Miller, *Lost Landmarks of Mississippi* (Jackson: University Press of Mississippi, 2002).

3. Information about Old Temple Beth Israel and a photograph of the building are included in Mary Carol Miller, *Lost Landmarks of Mississippi.*

4. Information about Old First Baptist Church of Greenwood and a photograph of the building are included in Mary Carol Miller, *Lost Landmarks of Mississippi.*

HISTORIC CHURCHES OF MISSISSIPPI

ABERDEEN

St. John's Episcopal Church, built in 1853, is one of several substantial brick Gothic Revival churches built for Episcopal congregations in Mississippi in the decade before the Civil War. Plans for this building were prepared by the rector, the Reverend Joseph Holt Ingraham, who oversaw its construction.

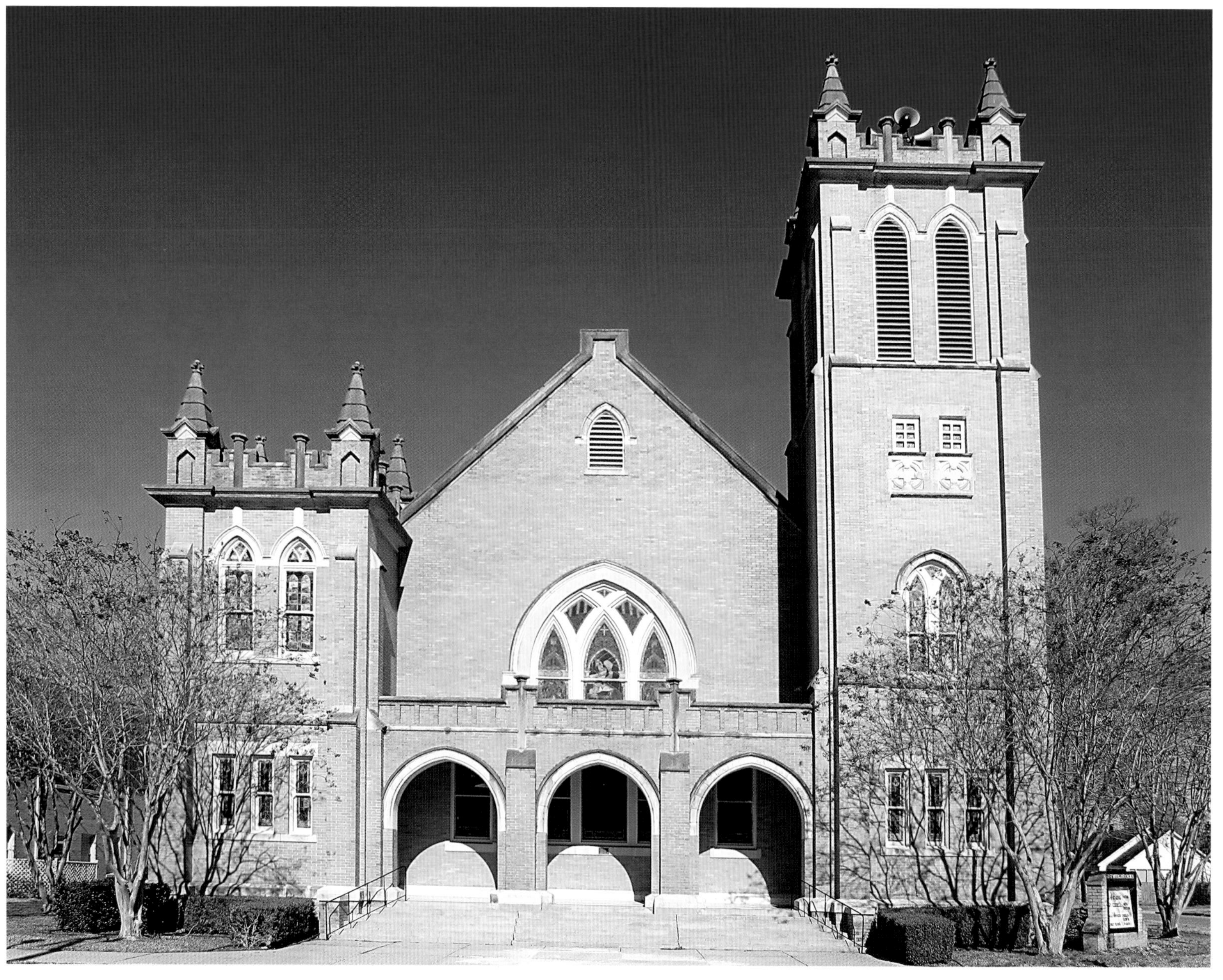

ABERDEEN

First United Methodist Church is a Gothic Revival auditorium-plan church built in 1915. The architect was Reuben Harrison Hunt of Chattanooga, Tennessee, who designed many other fine churches in Mississippi and throughout the South.

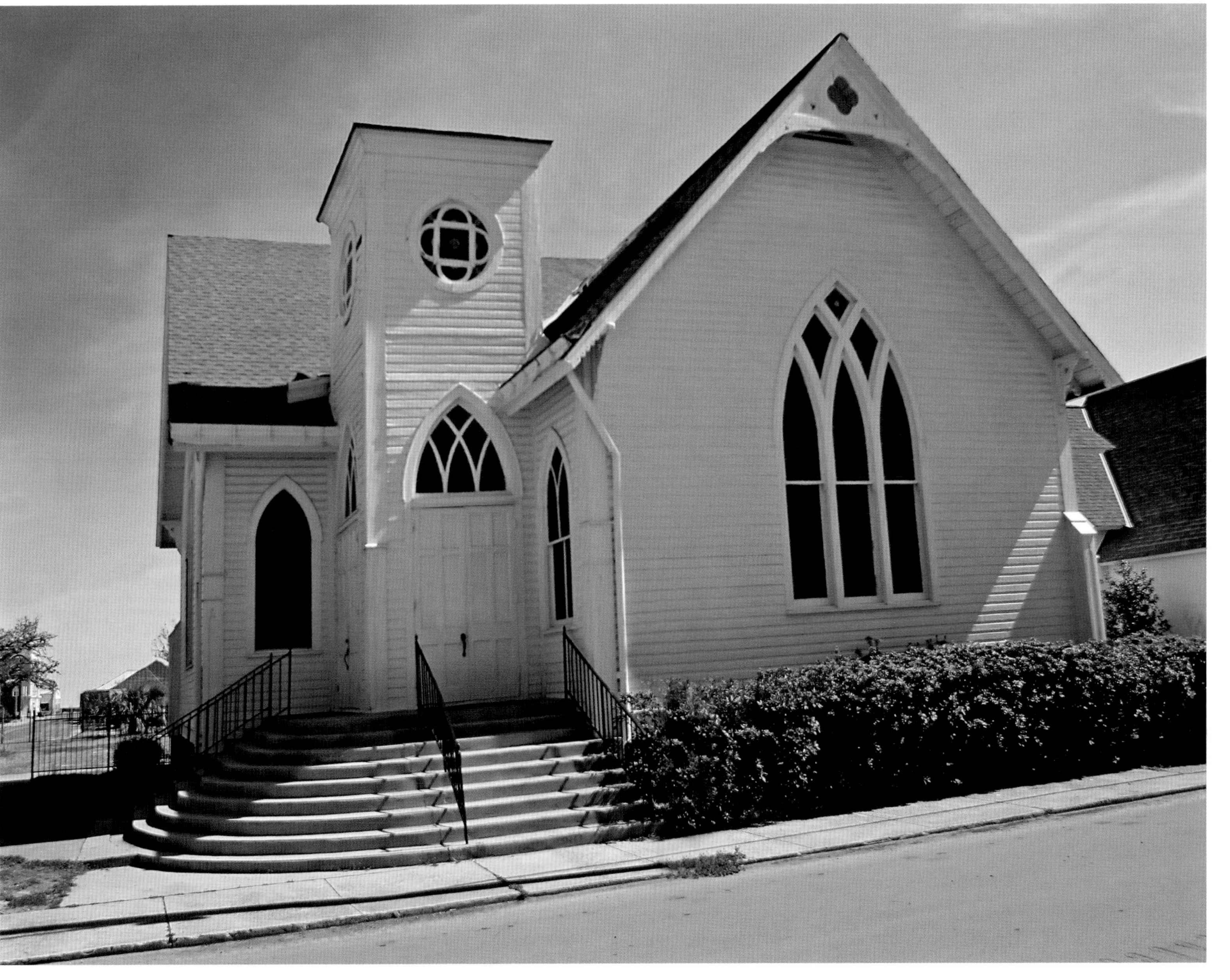

BAY ST. LOUIS

Built in 1895, *Main Street United Methodist Church* is a wood-frame vernacular Gothic Revival building. When Hurricane Katrina devastated Bay St. Louis on August 29, 2005, it damaged the church and tore off its steeple, but the building withstood the storm.

BILOXI

The Episcopal *Church of the Redeemer* was originally built in 1873–74. Jefferson Davis worshiped in this church while he resided at Beauvoir. After a new sanctuary was built in 1891, the old sanctuary was converted into a parish hall. When Hurricane Camille struck the Gulf Coast in 1969, it destroyed the 1891 sanctuary, leaving only the bell tower, but the original sanctuary survived the storm, and was subsequently returned to its original use as a house of worship. Although it endured Hurricane Camille, the venerable church was unable to withstand Hurricane Katrina, which destroyed both the original building and the tower of the second building.

BILOXI

The bell tower of the second Church of the Redeemer was all that remained after the 1891 building was destroyed by Hurricane Camille in 1969, but it, too, was destroyed when Hurricane Katrina struck the Gulf Coast in 2005.

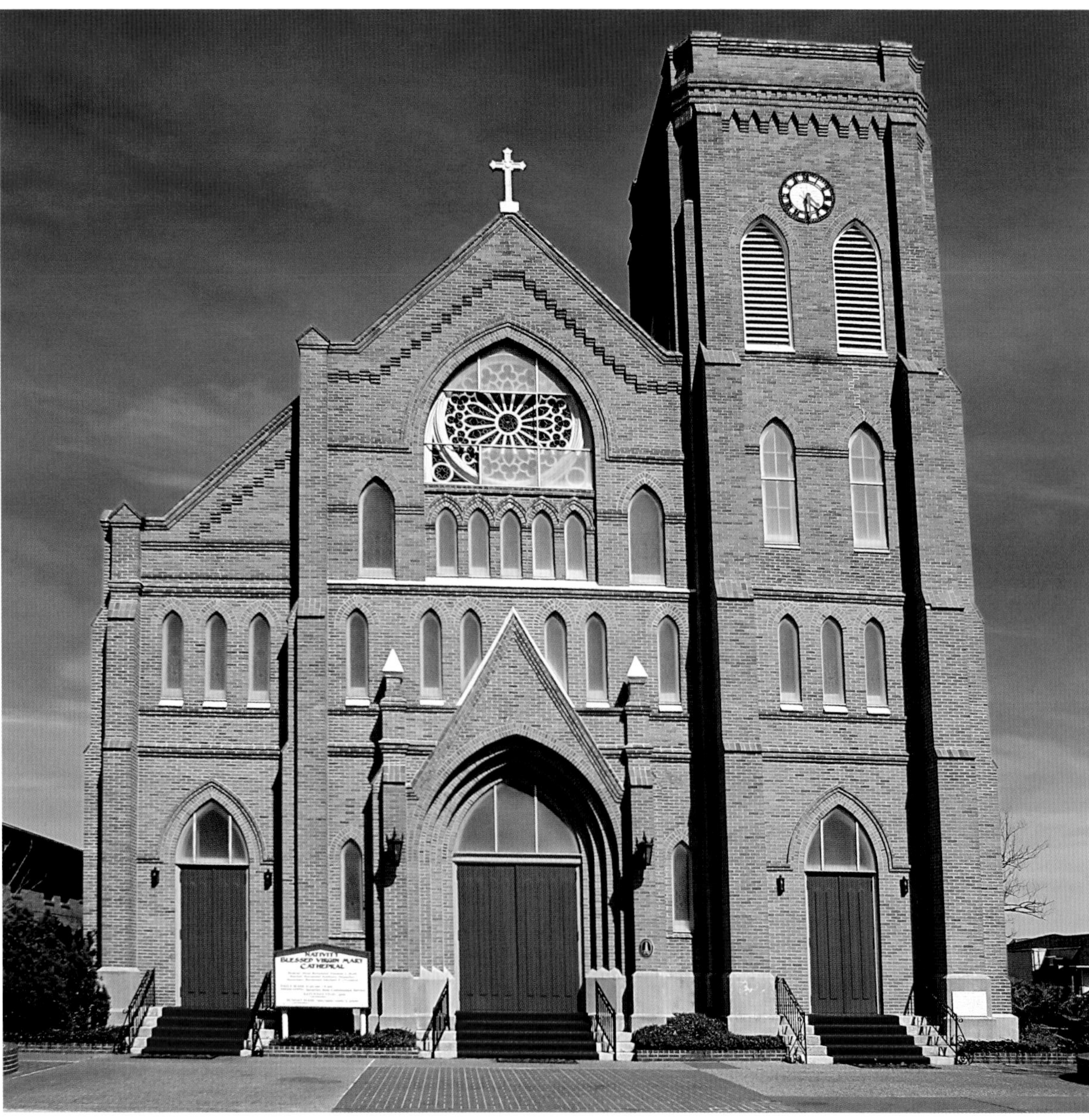

BILOXI

The finest Gothic Revival church on the Mississippi Gulf Coast is the Catholic *Cathedral of the Nativity of the Blessed Virgin Mary*, which was begun in 1901 and dedicated on September 14, 1902. The architect was Theodore Brune. This church became a cathedral in 1977 when the Diocese of Biloxi was created. The cathedral survived Hurricane Katrina with only minimal damage.

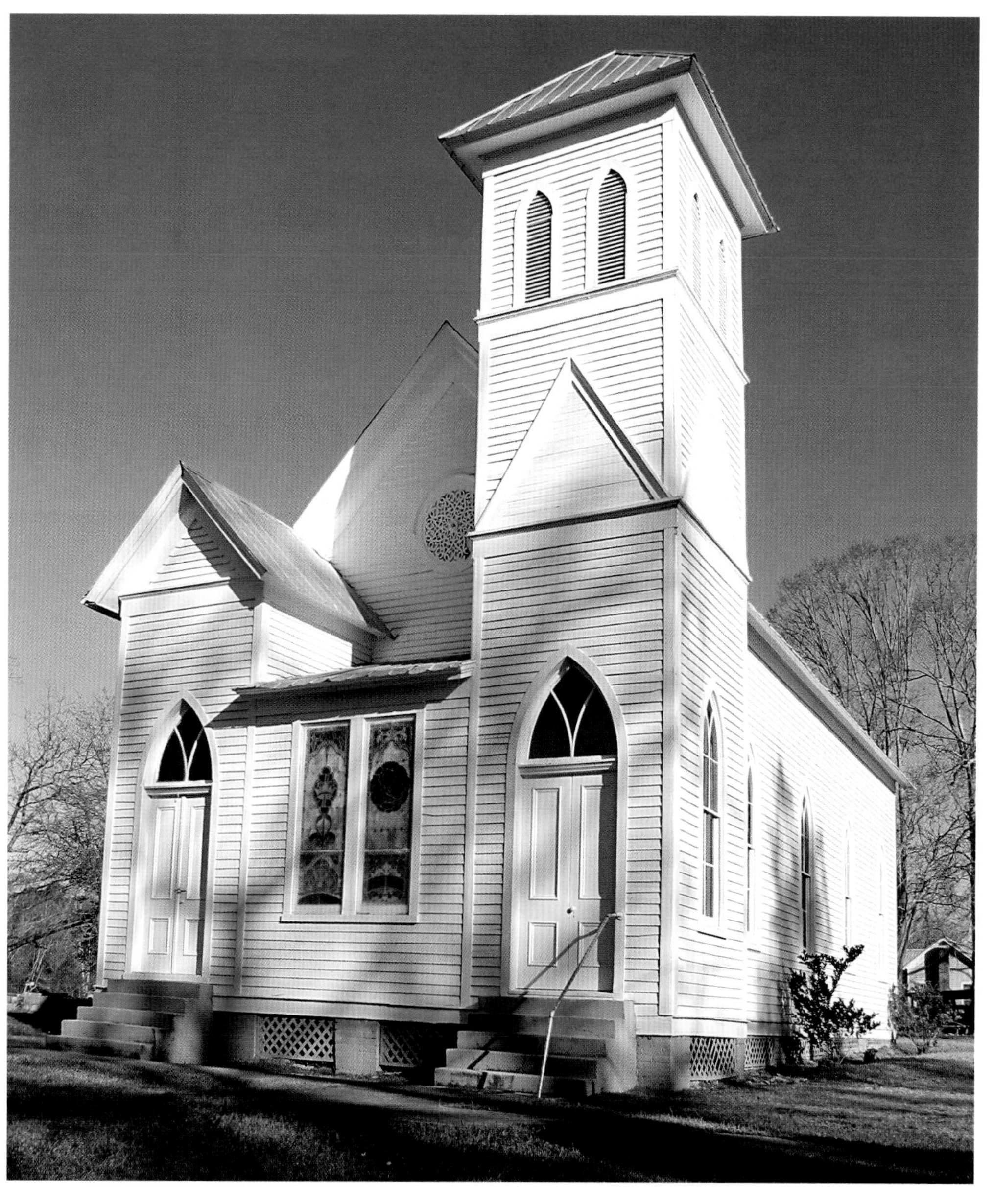

BOGUE CHITTO

Dating from 1883, *Bogue Chitto United Methodist Church* shows a local builder's free interpretation of "Carpenter Gothic" design.

BROOKHAVEN

Built in 1906–7, *First Presbyterian Church* is a Gothic Revival auditorium-plan church with four short, pyramidal-roofed towers, one at each corner.

BROOKHAVEN

The windows of First Presbyterian Church have unusually broad, low Gothic arches.

BROOKHAVEN

Temple B'nai Sholom is an eclectic Late Victorian wooden synagogue with Moorish-style windows in the front façade. It dates from 1896.

BROOKHAVEN

First United Methodist Church is an elegant Neoclassical Revival church built in 1917. Its architect was John Gaisford of Memphis, who also designed the Methodist church at Como.

BROOKHAVEN

A paneled tower surmounted by an octagonal steeple with a tall spire dominates the façade of *St. Francis of Assisi Catholic Church*, built in 1888. The entrance porch, with its steep gabled roof and iron posts, is a twentieth-century alteration.

BYHALIA

Byhalia United Methodist Church, built in 1906, was designed by Andrew Johnson, a Swedish-born architect and builder who designed many fine Late Victorian houses throughout North Mississippi. The steeple and porch are recent changes.

CANTON

First Baptist Church, built in 1918, is a Neoclassical Revival building distinguished by a projecting, semi-recessed tetrastyle (four-column) portico in the Ionic order.

CANTON

Located nearby at 228 South Liberty Street, *First United Methodist Church* is also a Neoclassical Revival building, constructed in 1922. Its façade is dominated by a projecting hexastyle (six-column) portico in the Tuscan order. The architect was Raymond B. Spencer, of Memphis, who also designed the First Baptist Church of Leland.

CANTON VICINITY

Sharon United Methodist Church, northeast of Canton, is a well-preserved example of the wooden vernacular churches built in rural areas throughout Mississippi in the later years of the nineteenth century.

CANTON VICINITY

The cemetery at Sharon contains numerous ornate nineteenth-century grave monuments.

CANTON

The finest antebellum Gothic Revival church of wooden construction in Mississippi is *Grace Episcopal Church*, built in 1853. Its plans were based on a design by Frank Wills, an English-born architect who lived and worked in New York and was one of the leading figures of the Ecclesiological movement in the United States. A cross positioned within a circular panel embellishes the tower (inset).

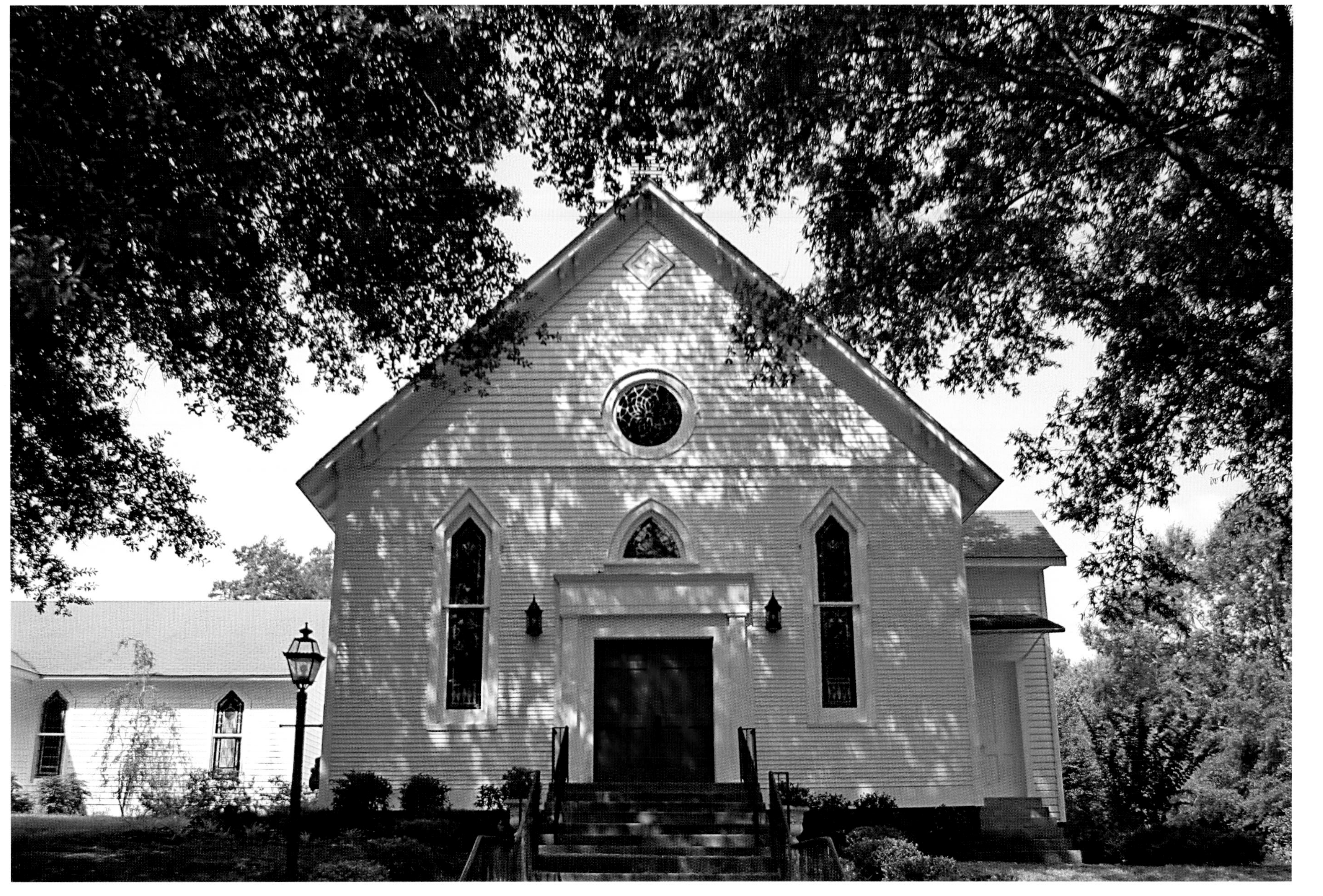

CARROLLTON

Carrollton United Methodist Church, built in 1885, combines Carpenter Gothic and Italianate features. The peaked windows of the front façade are a vernacular interpretation of Gothic pointed arches. The eaves of the front gable are ornamented with Italianate paired brackets similar to those at Holy Innocents Church in Como.

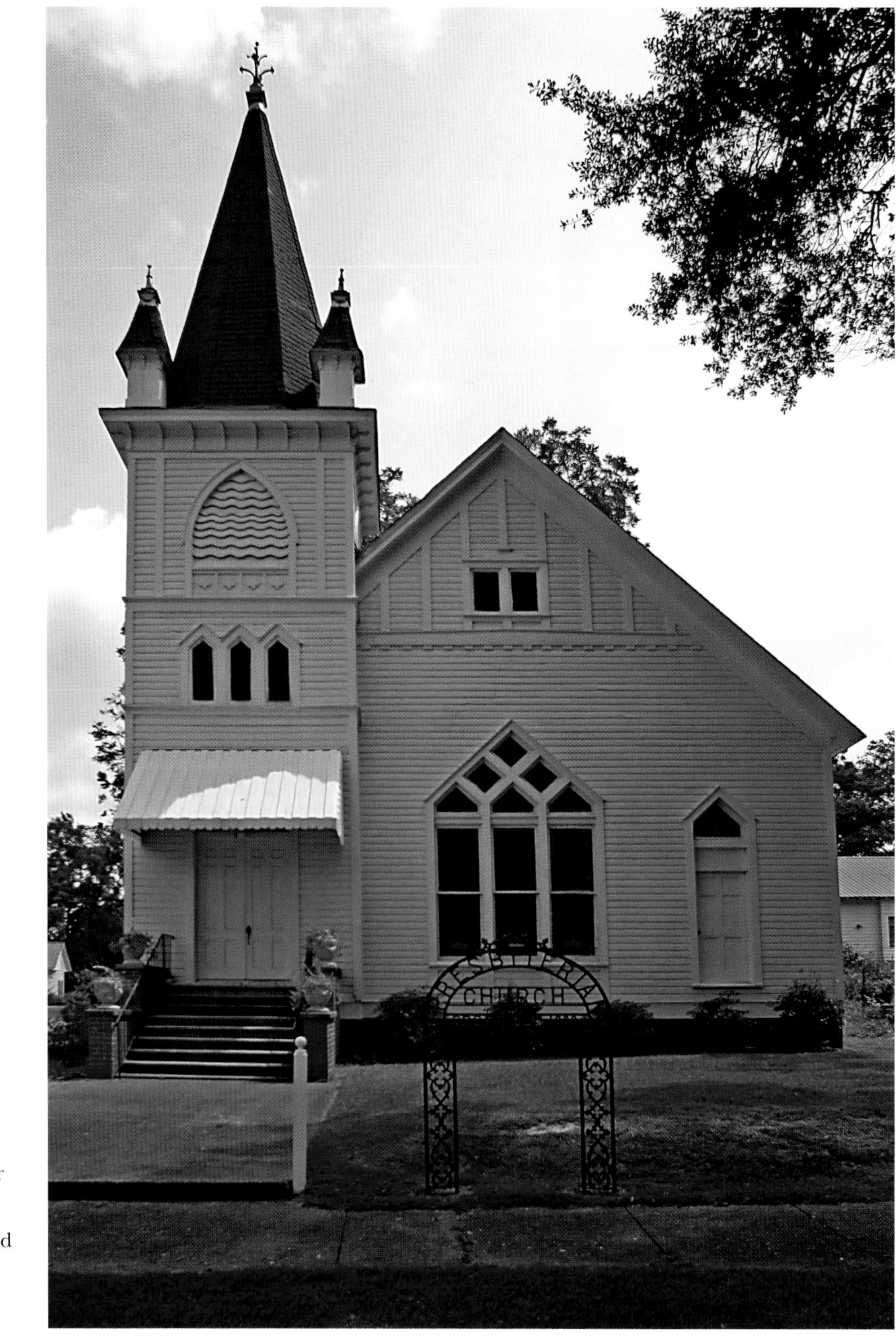

CARROLLTON

Carrollton Presbyterian Church is a Carpenter Gothic church built in 1897. The large window in the center of its façade has an angular peak instead of a curved pointed arch, with straight wooden framing substituted for curved Gothic tracery. The Methodist Church at Byhalia has a similar window.

CARROLLTON

The most prominent feature of the Carrollton Presbyterian Church is its tower, surmounted by a tall octagonal spire and four corner pinnacles.

CARROLLTON

Built in 1883, *Grace Episcopal Church* was designed by W. P. Wentworth of Boston, Massachusetts. Its eclectic design combines Gothic Revival and Stick style features.

CARROLLTON

The exposed framing that is characteristic of the Stick style is particularly evident in the bell tower of Grace Church.

CARROLLTON

Carrollton Baptist Church, built in 1894, is a brick Gothic Revival church with a corner tower. The slender spire atop its tower has been added in recent years.

CENTREVILLE VICINITY

Bethany Presbyterian Church, located east of Centreville in Amite County, was built about 1855. It is an exceptionally intact and refined example of a traditional vernacular church form distinguished by two identical entrances on its façade. Another example of this traditional form is Lebanon Presbyterian Church near Learned in Hinds County.

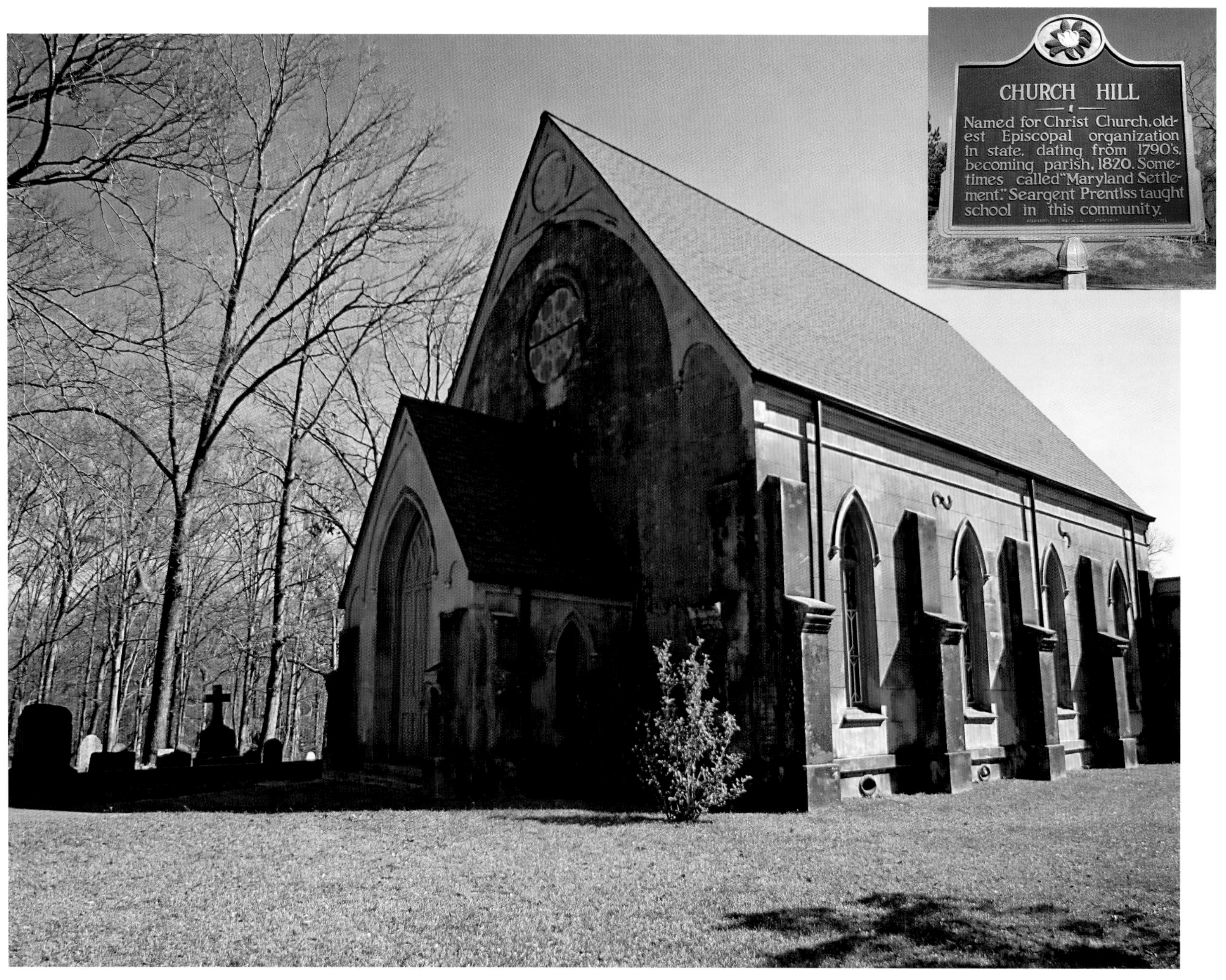

CHURCH HILL

Christ Church (Episcopal) in Jefferson County was built in 1857–58 on the site of an earlier church. It is a particularly intact example of a Gothic Revival church from the antebellum period. The brick walls are clad in stucco that has been scored to resemble stone blocks.

CHURCH HILL

The churchyard at Christ Church contains numerous nineteenth-century grave monuments.

CLARKSDALE

St. George's Episcopal Church, built in 1904, is similar in design to the Church of the Nativity in Greenwood and Immanuel Church in Winona, though its tower is less ornate.

CLARKSDALE

Clarksdale Baptist Church was built in 1919–20 after an earlier building was destroyed by fire in 1917. The brick Neoclassical Revival building with a projecting, semi-recessed tetrastyle portico in the Ionic order was designed by the Memphis architectural firm of Spencer & Abbott. (One of the architects, Raymond B. Spencer, also designed the First Methodist Church of Canton and the First Baptist Church of Leland.)

CLINTON

One of the finest surviving Greek Revival churches in Mississippi is *Provine Chapel* at Mississippi College. This temple-form brick building, raised upon a high basement, features an elegant hexastyle (six-column) portico in the Corinthian order. Built in 1859, it was designed by Jacob Larmour, who had practiced architecture in New York before coming to Mississippi in the early 1850s. He later worked in Indiana and Minnesota before moving in 1871 to Austin, Texas, where he had a long and successful architectural career.

CLINTON

The old sanctuary of *First Baptist Church* was built in 1923. This dignified Neoclassical Revival building is notable for its broad, semi-recessed, projecting hexastyle portico in the Ionic order. The architect was Reuben Harrison Hunt of Chattanooga, Tennessee, who designed many other fine churches in Mississippi and throughout the South.

COLUMBUS

First United Methodist Church was begun in 1860, but construction was interrupted by the Civil War. It was completed in 1866. Based on a design by the noted architect Samuel Sloan of Philadelphia, Pennsylvania, this building is a notable example of the Romanesque Revival style which was just beginning to appear in Mississippi on the eve of the Civil War.

COLUMBUS

Main Street Presbyterian Church, built in 1885, is particularly noteworthy for the contrasting brickwork that embellishes its walls, running in horizontal bands across its façade and accentuating its Gothic arches.

COLUMBUS

One of the finest surviving antebellum Gothic Revival churches in Mississippi, *St. Paul's Episcopal Church* was built in 1859.

COLUMBUS

The *Catholic Church of the Annunciation* was begun in 1863, but was not completed until 1878. It was designed by Father Jean Baptiste Mouton, a Catholic priest, who also designed Corpus Christi Catholic Church in Macon.

COLUMBUS

Built in 1908, *First Baptist Church* is a Gothic Revival auditorium-plan church designed by R. H. Hunt. With its two asymmetrical towers linked by an arcaded loggia, it is similar in appearance to First United Methodist Church in Aberdeen.

COMO

Como United Methodist Church, built in 1912, is an elegant Neoclassical Revival church designed by John Gaisford, of Memphis, who also designed the First United Methodist Church in Brookhaven.

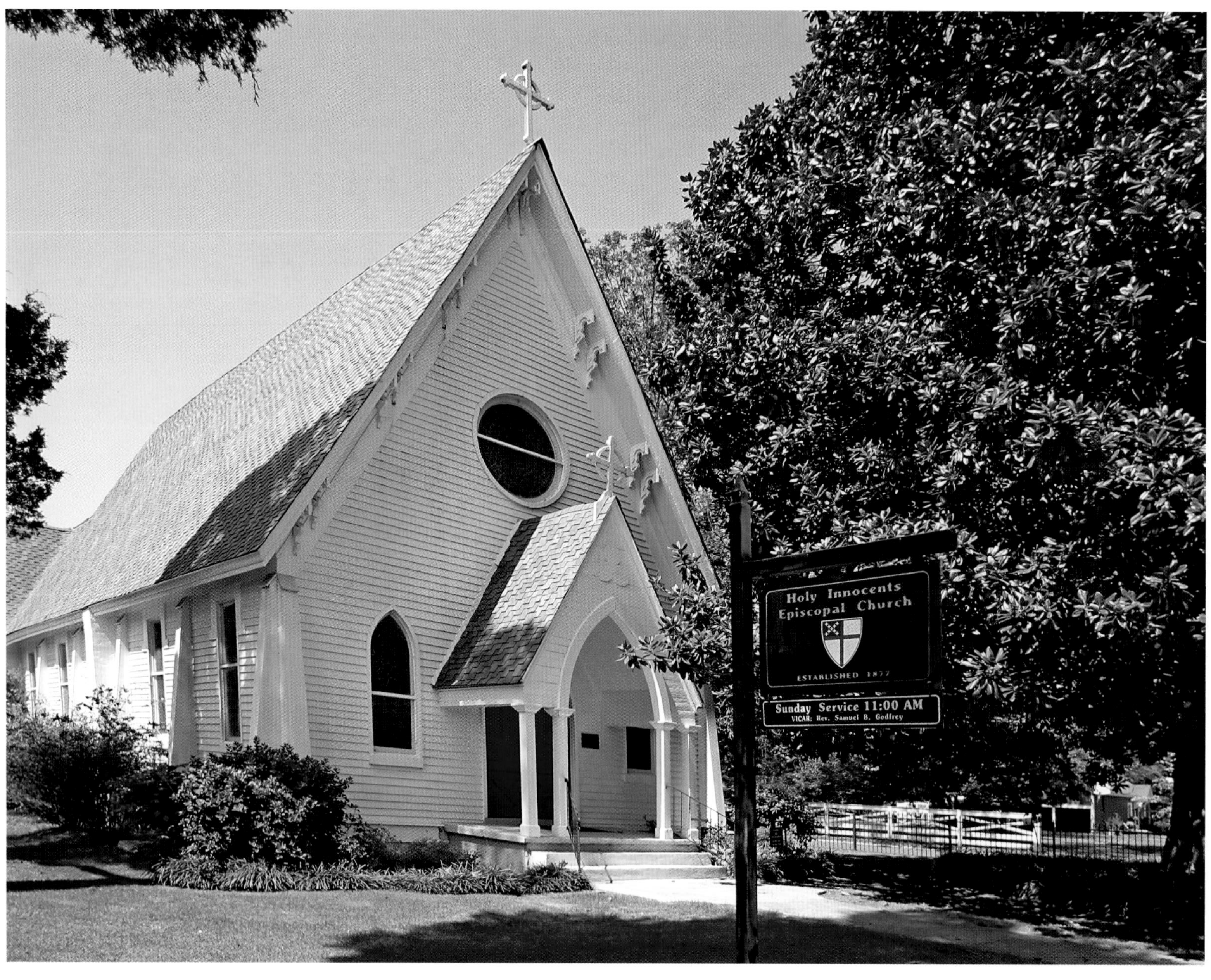

COMO

Holy Innocents Episcopal Church was built in 1872. Its architectural character is largely Gothic Revival, but its design also incorporates Italianate brackets in the front eaves. The architect of this building was James B. Cook, of Memphis, Tennessee, who also designed the Church of Our Savior in Iuka.

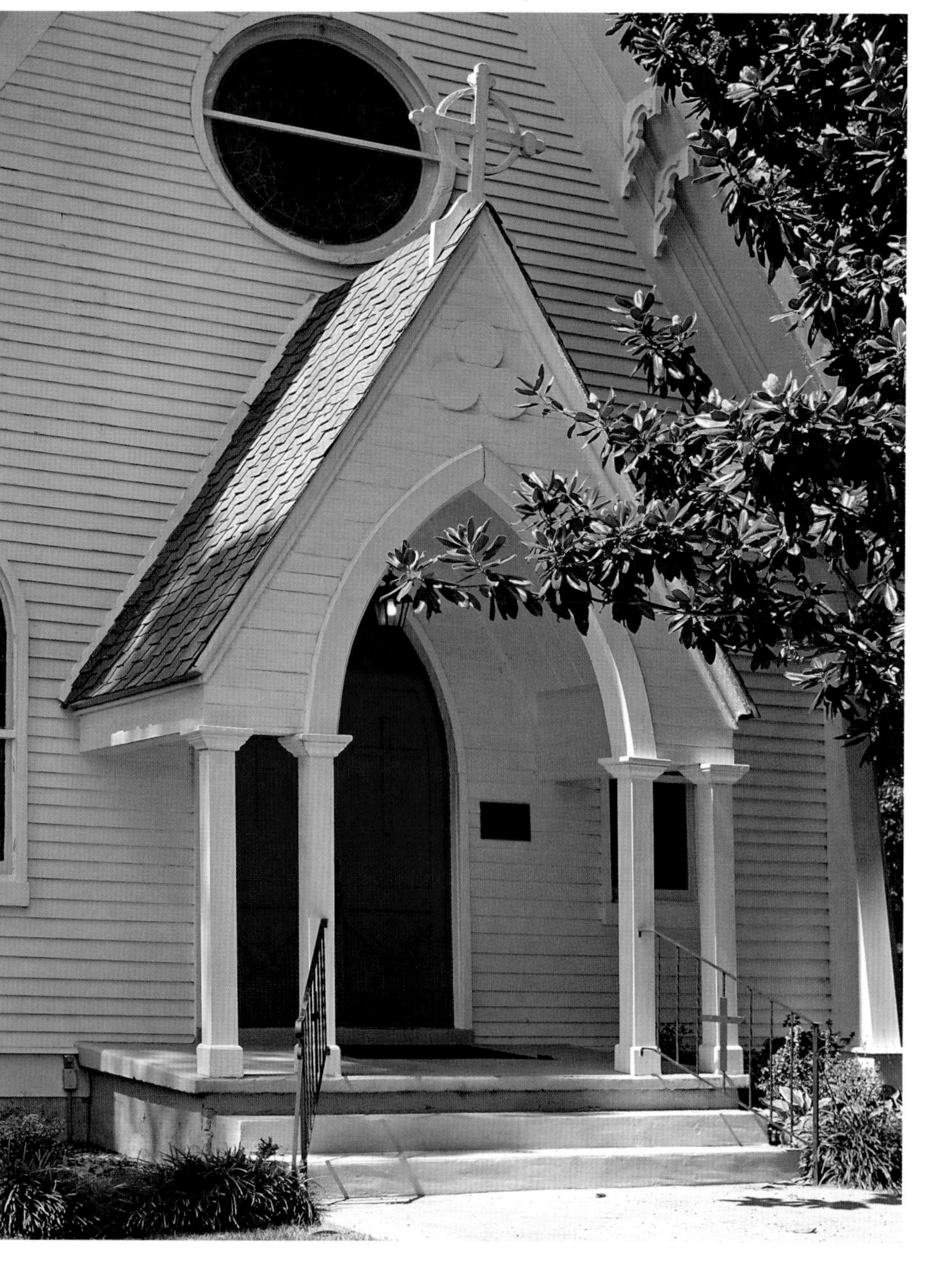

COMO

The Gothic pointed arch of the porch is supported by four colonnettes (miniature columns).

COMO VICINITY

Located east of Como in a rural area of Panola County, *Fredonia United Methodist Church* was built in 1848. Its design is a combination of vernacular Greek Revival and Gothic Revival features.

ENTERPRISE

St. Mary's Episcopal Church is a small Carpenter Gothic church built in 1874.

GREENVILLE

One of the largest and finest Gothic Revival churches in the Mississippi Delta region is *St. Joseph's Catholic Church*, constructed in 1908.

GREENVILLE

Hebrew Union Temple, built in 1906, is an elaborate Classical Revival synagogue very similar in appearance to Temple B'nai Israel in Natchez. It was designed by the same architect, H. A. Overbeck of Dallas, Texas.

GREENWOOD

During the late 1890s and early 1900s, the prolific architect R. H. Hunt designed many Romanesque Revival auditorium-plan churches throughout the South, including *First United Methodist Church*, built in 1898.

GREENWOOD

A large, square corner tower is a typical feature of the Romanesque Revival churches designed by R. H. Hunt, but each of his towers is different. They vary in height, in the number and placement of openings, and in the arrangement of belt-courses and moldings. This tower is subtly different from the similar tower at Moore Memorial United Methodist Church in Winona.

GREENWOOD

The Episcopal *Church of the Nativity* was built in 1902. This eclectic Gothic Revival building with classical detailing on its tower is almost identical to Immanuel Episcopal Church in Winona, though the plan is reversed.

GREENWOOD

The present sanctuary of *First Presbyterian Church* was built in 1925–26, immediately adjacent to the old sanctuary, which had been built in 1904. The old sanctuary originally had an auditorium-plan interior with radial seating on a diagonal axis. The present sanctuary's rectangular plan with a central processional aisle is characteristic of the more formal Neo-Gothic churches of the 1920s and 1930s. The façade, with its centrally placed entrance, gives an external expression of the center-aisle plan.

GRENADA

Built in 1905, *First Presbyterian Church* is a very intact auditorium-plan Gothic Revival church with radial seating on a center axis.

GRENADA

Two towers of uneven height dominate the façade of First Presbyterian Church. The smaller tower is capped by a pyramidal roof, and the taller tower has a steeper and more complex spire. The towers are similar in arrangement to those on the Methodist church at Okolona.

GRENADA

All Saints Episcopal Church is a well-preserved Late Victorian Gothic Revival church built in 1889–90.

GULFPORT

Handsboro Presbyterian Church on Pass Road was built in 1891. It served the community of Handsboro, which was later annexed into Gulfport. This building survived Hurricane Katrina with relatively little damage, though (like Main Street United Methodist Church in Bay St. Louis) it lost its steeple.

HATTIESBURG

Main Street United Methodist Church is a Gothic Revival auditorium-plan church built in 1909–10.

HATTIESBURG

Atop the tower of Main Street United Methodist Church is a pyramidal spire with a square pinnacle at each corner.

HATTIESBURG

Bay Street Presbyterian Church, built in 1907–8, is one of several notable Romanesque Revival auditorium-plan churches in Mississippi designed by R. H. Hunt.

HATTIESBURG

A distinctive feature of several of R. H. Hunt's Romanesque Revival churches is a slender octagonal pinnacle on the main façade in a position opposite the tower, as can be seen on Bay Street Presbyterian Church. First United Methodist Church in Greenwood also has a similar pinnacle.

HATTIESBURG

Completed in 1912, *Trinity Episcopal Church* was designed by the Reverend William Atmore-Simpson, who was rector of the church at that time.

HAZLEHURST

First Baptist Church, designed by R. H. Hunt, was built in 1926. This fine Neoclassical Revival church is a "temple-form" building, in which the portico extends the full width of the façade and is contained under the same gabled roof as the main rectangular body of the building, so that the building has the shape of an ancient Roman temple. Other "temple-form" Neoclassical Revival churches are First United Methodist in Brookhaven and Galloway Memorial United Methodist in Jackson.

HOLLY SPRINGS

(Old) *St. Joseph's Catholic Church* (now called the *Church of the Yellow Fever Martyrs*) was originally built in the early 1840s as the first building of Christ Episcopal Church. It was sold to the Catholics in 1857 and moved to its present location, where it served the Catholic parish until a new St. Joseph's church was completed in 1981.

HOLLY SPRINGS

Built in 1923, *First Baptist Church* is one of several Neoclassical Revival churches in Mississippi that share a similar design featuring a projecting, semi-recessed portico with entrances located in the side walls of the recessed area of the portico. Other churches with this design include Clarksdale Baptist, First Presbyterian and First Methodist in Starkville, and First Baptist in Canton. Each of these buildings, however, has subtle differences.

HOLLY SPRINGS

First Presbyterian Church is one of four Romanesque Revival churches in Mississippi begun on the eve of the Civil War. Construction began in 1860 but was not completed until 1869.

IUKA

Built in 1873, the *Church of Our Savior* was designed by James B. Cook, an English-born architect who was residing at that time in Memphis. Cook also designed Holy Innocents Episcopal Church in Como. The Church of Our Savior was built for an Episcopal congregation but now serves as a community chapel. The significance of the Church of Our Savior is recognized by a State Historical Marker (inset).

JACKSON

St. Andrew's Episcopal Cathedral is located at 305 East Capitol Street in downtown Jackson, directly across the street from the Governor's Mansion. The present sanctuary, constructed in 1903, is the third for St. Andrew's, which was organized in 1839. The architect was P. H. Weathers of Jackson, who also designed the nearby Catholic Cathedral of St. Peter the Apostle.

JACKSON

The tower of St. Andrew's Episcopal Cathedral is crowned with ornate pinnacles.

JACKSON

The chapel at the Mississippi Agriculture and Forestry Museum was originally built as the *Episcopal Church of the Epiphany* at Hermanville in Claiborne County about 1887. By about 1982, the congregation had become inactive. The building was moved to the museum complex and opened as the museum chapel in 1985.

JACKSON

The stained-glass window that illuminates the altar is located in the center of the south wall. The pointed arch of the window opening is called an equilateral arch because it is formed from the points of an equilateral triangle.

JACKSON

One of the largest and finest Neoclassical Revival churches in Mississippi is *Galloway Memorial United Methodist Church*, designed by R. H. Hunt and built from 1913 to 1915. The temple-form building has an octastyle (eight-column) portico in the Tuscan order extending across the entire façade.

LAUREL

First-Trinity Presbyterian Church was built in 1924–25. Originally named First Presbyterian Church, it took the name First-Trinity after the congregation merged with the Trinity Presbyterian Church congregation in 1992. Within this building's rather austere exterior is an exceptionally elegant early twentieth-century Neo-Gothic interior, as well as one of the state's finest pipe organs.

LAUREL

Built in 1914, *St. John's Episcopal Church* is a fine Romanesque Revival building designed by Frank A. Colby, a New York architect. The contractor was I. C. Garber of Jackson, who also built Galloway Memorial United Methodist Church in Jackson and Immanuel Church in Winona, among many other substantial buildings around the state.

LAUREL

Above the entrance of St. John's is a large, circular stained-glass window, bordered by terra-cotta panels representing the Four Evangelists.

LEAKESVILLE VICINITY

Dating from 1906–8, *Vernal Presbyterian Church* is located in the rural community of Vernal, south of Leakesville in Greene County.

LEARNED

Learned United Methodist Church is a modest vernacular church built in 1891–92.

LEARNED VICINITY

Lebanon Presbyterian Church, located near Learned in Hinds County, is a simple vernacular church with two entrances in its gable end. It was originally constructed in 1854 and was renovated early in the twentieth century.

LEARNED VICINITY

On the grounds of Lebanon Church, as at many nineteenth-century rural churches, is a cemetery.

LELAND

Built in 1922–23, *First Baptist Church* is an elegant Neoclassical Revival building with a projecting tetrastyle (four-column) portico in the Tuscan order. The architect was Raymond B. Spencer, who also designed First United Methodist Church in Canton.

LELAND

Leland United Methodist Church is one of the few Mission Style churches in Mississippi. It was built in 1923–24.

LEXINGTON

St. Mary's Episcopal Church is a well-preserved Carpenter Gothic church built in 1900.
Its most distinctive feature is its unusual octagonal corner tower.

LEXINGTON

The tower of St. Mary's at Lexington is capped by an octagonal spire.

LEXINGTON

Two asymmetrical corner towers dominate the façade of *Asia Baptist Church*, completed in 1908.

LEXINGTON

The steeple atop the taller of the two towers of Asia Baptist Church has a pyramidal spire with a square pinnacle at each corner. The towers of several other churches depicted in this book have similar steeples.

LEXINGTON

First United Methodist Church is a brick Gothic Revival church constructed in 1897.

LIBERTY

Liberty Presbyterian Church, built about 1850, has an austere Greek Revival character.

LIBERTY VICINITY

Berwick Baptist Church, located southwest of Liberty in Amite County, was built about 1901. It is unusual among Mississippi's rural Carpenter Gothic churches in having its entrance positioned on one of the longer side walls of the building instead of in the front gable end or in a corner tower. It shares this feature with the former Church of the Epiphany of Hermanville, which is now located at the Mississippi Agriculture and Forestry Museum in Jackson.

MACON

Corpus Christi Catholic Church, built in 1874, was designed by Father Jean Baptiste Mouton, a Catholic priest who also designed the Church of the Annunciation in Columbus.

MACON

First Baptist Church of Macon is a Gothic Revival auditorium-plan church built in 1909.

MACON

The mullions of this stained-glass window form an interlaced pattern, called tracery, that is a characteristic feature of Gothic architecture.

MADISON VICINITY

One of the most notable Gothic Revival churches built in Mississippi before the Civil War is *Chapel of the Cross*, near Madison, which was begun about 1850 and consecrated in 1852. Its design is a modification of a published design by Frank Wills, one of the leading architects of the Ecclesiological movement.

MADISON VICINITY

Several of the family plots in the cemetery at Chapel of the Cross are surrounded by ornate cast-iron fences.

MADISON VICINITY

These ornate nineteenth-century grave monuments are located in the cemetery at Chapel of the Cross.

MAGNOLIA

The Episcopal *Church of Our Redeemer* is a modest vernacular building with simplified Gothic detailing, built about 1875. Along the side walls (not visible in this photograph) are angular peaked windows like those at Church of the Good Shepherd in Terry.

MAGNOLIA

Magnolia Presbyterian Church, a vernacular Gothic Revival church of wood construction, was built in 1881–82.

McCOMB

J. J. White Memorial Presbyterian Church, located at the intersection of Delaware Avenue and Broadway at the head of Main Street, occupies the most visually prominent position in downtown McComb. Designed by Kramer & Lindsley, architects, this brick Gothic Revival building was constructed in 1921 to replace an earlier wooden structure, which was moved a short distance away to be used by the Christian Church.

McCOMB

St. Alphonsus Catholic Church, built in 1922, exemplifies a mode of Romanesque Revival architecture popular during the 1910s and 1920s that was inspired by the medieval churches of Italy.

McCOMB

The twin towers of St. Alphonsus Catholic Church are embellished with decorative brickwork in the form of "blind arcades." The arches of the belfry openings are accented with darker-toned bricks.

MERIDIAN

Built in 1912, *First Presbyterian Church* is a Gothic Revival auditorium-plan church with radial seating on a diagonal axis. Its architect was P. J. Krouse of Meridian.

MERIDIAN

With its rough stone walls and boldly jutting buttresses, Meridian's First Presbyterian Church is an unusually robust, vigorous interpretation of Gothic architecture.

MERIDIAN

Built in 1902, *St. Paul's Episcopal Church* is a brick Gothic Revival church with a projecting gable-roofed entrance vestibule.

MERIDIAN

The façade of *St. Patrick's Catholic Church* has a lively variety of arched openings and blind arches. The Gothic Revival church, built in 1886, was designed by Alfred J. R. E. Zucker, a German-born architect who also designed the Ricks Memorial Library in Yazoo City.

NATCHEZ

Originally built in 1828–29, with additional work in the 1830s and 1850s, *First Presbyterian Church* has both Federal and Greek Revival stylistic features. Of particular interest in the interior are the hinged doors on the pews.

NATCHEZ

The upper tier of the steeple of First Presbyterian Church is an octagonal cupola surmounted by a dome. Similar Federal-style octagonal cupolas can be seen on the Presbyterian Church at Rodney and several early churches in Woodville.

NATCHEZ

The oldest and most historic Catholic church in Mississippi is *St. Mary Basilica,* which was begun in 1842 and was essentially completed in 1859. St. Mary was designed by Robert Cary Long of Baltimore, Maryland, and it is strikingly similar to his design for St. Alphonsus Catholic Church in Baltimore. The supervising architect of St. Mary was James Hardie of Natchez. St. Mary served as the Cathedral of the Diocese of Natchez (later Natchez-Jackson) until 1977, when the diocese became the Diocese of Jackson, and St. Peter's in Jackson became the cathedral. In September 1998 St. Mary was designated a Basilica in recognition of its historical importance.

NATCHEZ

The tower of St. Mary Basilica is topped with pinnacles linked by an open balustrade, behind which rises a tall, very slender octagonal spire.

NATCHEZ

Trinity Episcopal Church is one of the oldest church buildings in Mississippi. Originally built in 1822 in the Federal style, it was remodeled in 1838, and the Greek Revival portico was added.

NATCHEZ VICINITY

Kingston United Methodist Church is located in the Kingston community southeast of Natchez. Built in 1856–57, it is a very well-preserved rural Greek Revival church. Sheltering the entrance is a pedimented distyle (two-column) portico.

NATCHEZ

The completion of *Temple B'nai Israel* in 1905 heralded the return of the Classical tradition to religious architecture in Mississippi after a lapse of nearly thirty years. The synagogue is a richly detailed essay in the ornate Beaux Arts mode of Classical Revival architecture. The architect of Temple B'nai Israel was H. A. Overbeck, of Dallas, Texas. The Jewish synagogue in Greenville, Hebrew Union Temple, built in 1906, is very similar in appearance.

NATCHEZ

Above the front entrance of Temple B'nai Israel is a stained-glass transom set within a semi-circular arch.

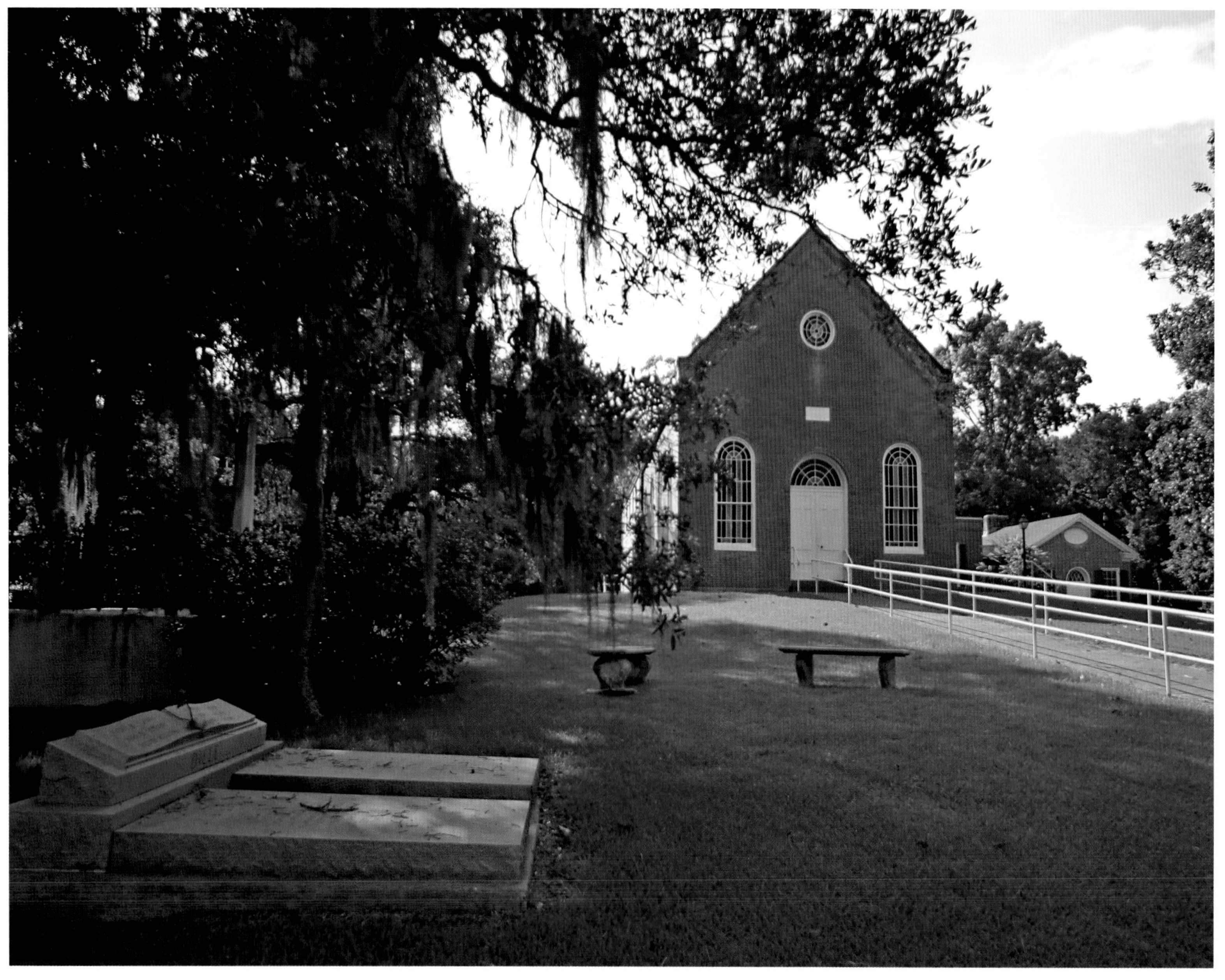

NATCHEZ VICINITY

Located a short distance north of Natchez on Pine Ridge Road, *Pine Ridge Presbyterian Church* was built in 1909 to replace an earlier church, dating from 1828, that was destroyed by a tornado in 1908.

NATCHEZ VICINITY

The picturesque cemetery at Pine Ridge Presbyterian Church contains some fine nineteenth-century burial monuments.

NATCHEZ VICINITY

Carmel Presbyterian Church, located southeast of Natchez, is a vernacular Greek Revival church dating from 1854. Its design is a scaled-down and simplified interpretation of the design of First Presbyterian Church in Natchez.

NATCHEZ VICINITY

Built in 1828, *Washington United Methodist Church* originally had a two-story height interior with galleries, but the ceiling was lowered when the building was remodeled in 1902.

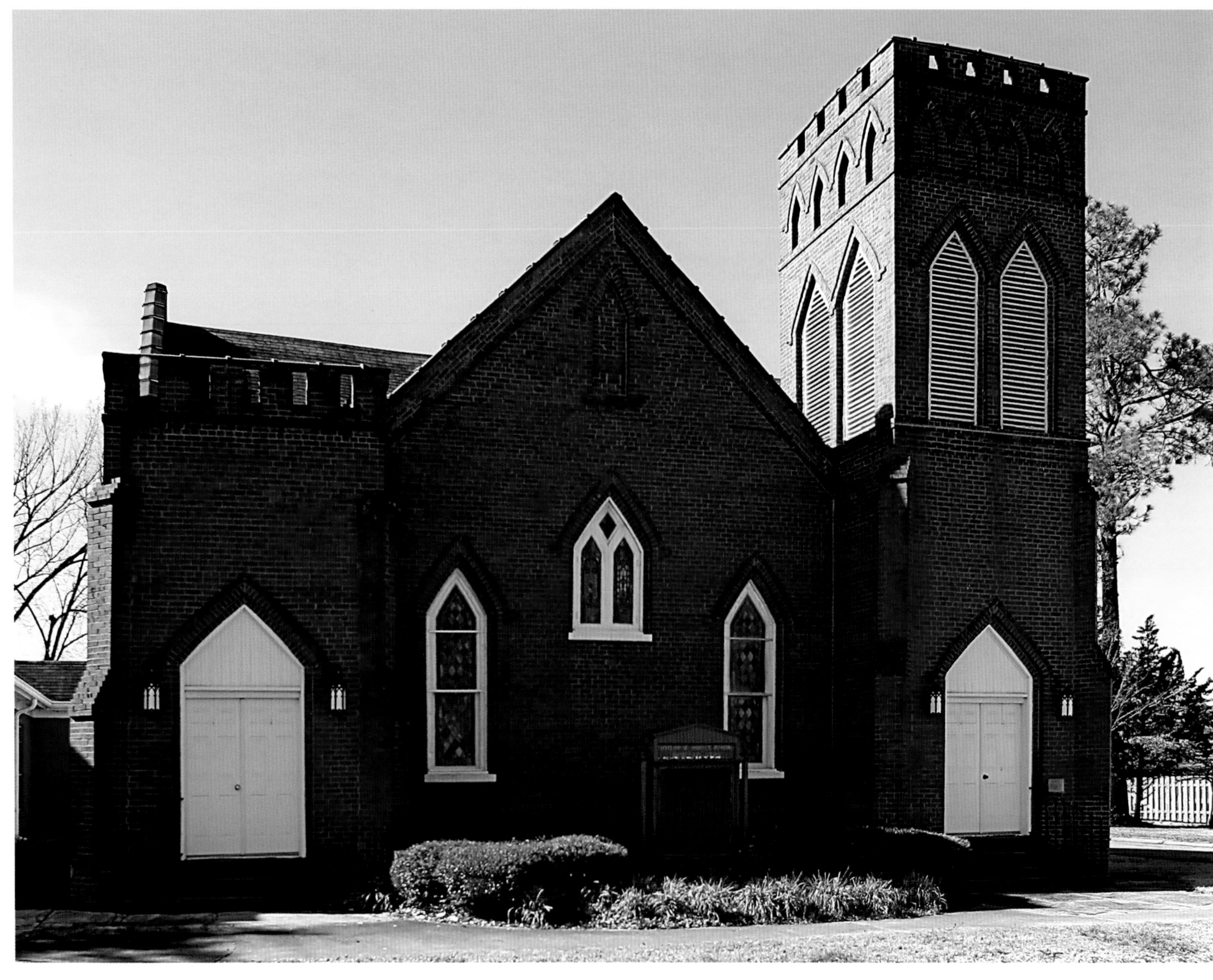

NEW ALBANY

Cleveland Street Associate Reformed Presbyterian Church, built in 1905, exhibits an austere, simplified interpretation of the Gothic Revival.

OCEAN SPRINGS

The old sanctuary of *Ocean Springs Presbyterian Church* is a simple vernacular church building erected about 1886.

OCEAN SPRINGS

St. John's Episcopal Church was built in 1892. Its design was based on that of the Church of Ascension at Rockville Center, Long Island, New York, designed by Manly N. Cutter, a New York architect.

OKOLONA

The design of *Grace Episcopal Church,* built in 1908, was patterned after that of the now long-vanished St. Columb's Chapel in Jackson, which served briefly as the bishop's chapel from 1894 to 1902. The Church of the Resurrection in Starkville is also based on the design of St. Columb's Chapel.

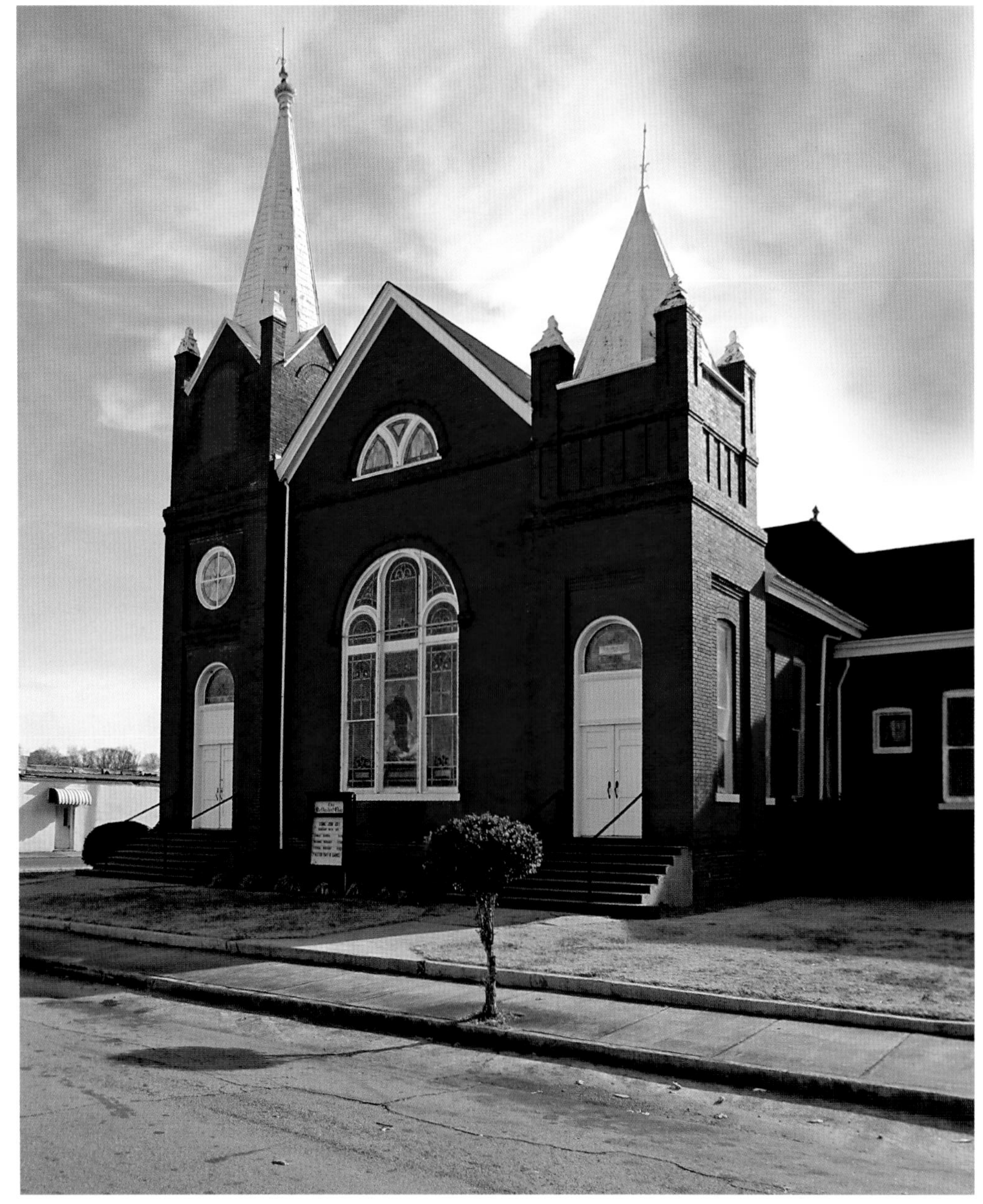

OKOLONA

Okolona United Methodist Church is a Romanesque Revival church built in 1907–8.

OXFORD VICINITY

College Hill Presbyterian Church is located in the College Hill community, north of Oxford in Lafayette County. The congregation of this church was organized in 1836 as Ebenezer Church. The name was changed to College Church in 1841, in reference to the nearby North Mississippi College, which operated from 1840 to 1860. The historic sanctuary building of the church was constructed in 1846.

OXFORD

Built in 1880, *First Presbyterian Church* has an eclectic Romanesque Revival character with some Italianate features. A comparison of this church with the Church of the Holy Trinity in Vicksburg and First United Methodist Church in Greenwood gives an indication of the great variety that was encompassed by the stylistic designation "Romanesque" during the Late Victorian period.

OXFORD

The tower is capped by an unusual roof, square in plan, but with double-curving slopes so that it is somewhat bell-shaped, and supported by a bracketed cornice. This is not a Romanesque design, but seems more evocative of the Second Empire style, much like the mansard-roofed towers on some High Victorian Italianate residences such as the Steers-Sykes-Locke House in Columbus.

OXFORD

Erected in 1857–58, *St. Peter's Episcopal Church* is one of several substantial Gothic Revival churches built in Mississippi before the Civil War. The tower was added in 1893.

OXFORD

Atop the tower of St. Peter's is a tall, slender octagonal spire.

POCAHONTAS

Built in 1902, *Pocahontas United Methodist Church*, located northwest of Jackson, is a well-preserved vernacular Carpenter Gothic church with a corner tower.

PONTOTOC

One of the many churches in Mississippi designed by R. H. Hunt, *First United Methodist Church* is a Romanesque Revival building constructed in 1910.

PONTOTOC

Built in 1915, *First Presbyterian Church* has a distinctive Prairie Style character.

PORT GIBSON VICINITY

Sacred Heart Catholic Church was originally built at Rodney in 1867–68. In 1983 it was moved to Grand Gulf Military Park near Port Gibson and restored to serve as the park's chapel.

PORT GIBSON

Built in 1891, *Temple Gemiluth Chassed* is the oldest surviving Jewish synagogue in Mississippi. Designed by Bartlett & Budemeyer, architects, of St. Louis, Missouri, the temple is a very rare example of Moorish-inspired architecture in Mississippi.

PORT GIBSON

The tower of Temple Gemiluth Chassed is given a Moorish character by ventilators in the shape of "keyhole" arches and a square-plan ogee-curved "onion" dome.

PORT GIBSON

One of the few substantial Roman Catholic churches constructed in Mississippi before the Civil War was *St. Joseph Catholic Church*, which was built in 1850–51. Its architect was Michael Foley of St. Louis, Missouri. Sunlight filtering though the blue glass of the windows gives the sanctuary an ethereal ambience.

PORT GIBSON

Begun in 1858 and completed in 1860, *First United Methodist Church* is one of two antebellum Romanesque Revival churches in Port Gibson.

PORT GIBSON

First Presbyterian Church, built in 1859, is an elegant and well-preserved Romanesque Revival church. This building and the nearby Methodist Church are the only two Romanesque Revival churches in the state that were completed before the outbreak of the Civil War.

PORT GIBSON

The First Presbyterian Church is widely known for the "hand pointing to heaven" atop its tall steeple.

PORT GIBSON VICINITY

Rocky Springs Methodist Church is located just off the Natchez Trace Parkway, north of Port Gibson in Claiborne County. Built in 1837, it is a well-preserved vernacular brick church with twin entrances.

PORT GIBSON VICINITY

Rocky Springs Methodist Church is noted for its picturesque cemetery, draped with Spanish moss.

RAYMOND

Immaculate Conception Catholic Church was built in 1885.

RAYMOND

Above the front door of Immaculate Conception Catholic Church is a round-arched stained-glass window.

RAYMOND

St. Mark's Episcopal Church, built in 1854, is a very intact antebellum church that exhibits a combination of Gothic Revival and Greek Revival features. (Fredonia United Methodist Church near Como has a similar combination of Gothic Revival and Greek Revival features, as does Mt. Zion Baptist Church at Rodney.)

RODNEY

Mt. Zion Baptist Church, believed to date from the 1850s, exhibits an interesting combination of styles. The pointed arches of the door and windows are Gothic, the pedimented gable is Greek Revival, and the octagonal cupola, capped by a dome, is a feature of the Federal style.

RODNEY

Built in 1832, *Rodney Presbyterian Church* is Mississippi's most distinctive Federal-style church. Its stylistic character is particularly evident in the elliptical fanlights over the front doors, which can be compared to similar fanlight transoms on some of the state's finer Federal-style houses, such as Rosalie in Natchez and the Lewis House in Woodville.

RODNEY

The round-arched windows of the upper façade retain their original louvered shutters. Mortared into place above this window is a cannonball that struck the building when Rodney was bombarded by Union forces during the Civil War.

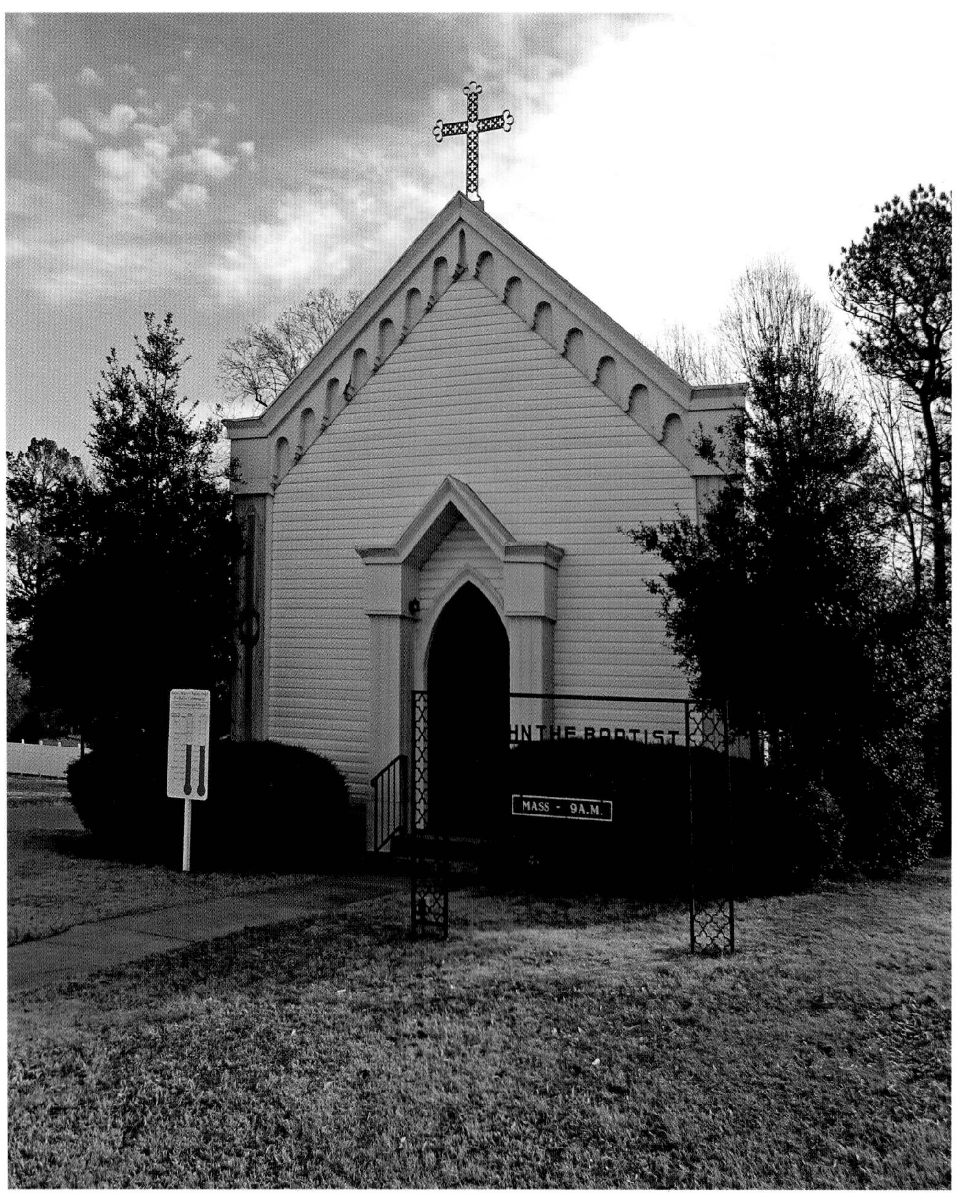

SARDIS

St. John the Baptist Catholic Church, built in 1891, is a vernacular church of wood construction with Gothic and Romanesque detailing. Of particular interest is the scalloped cornice, which is an interpretation, in wood, of the scalloped corbel detailing that ornaments the cornices of some Romanesque churches, as can be seen on the façade of St. Mary's Episcopal Church in Vicksburg and on the tower of First Presbyterian Church in Port Gibson.

SHUBUTA

Distinguished by three towers, each capped by a spire, *Shubuta United Methodist Church*, built in 1891, is an elaborately detailed Carpenter Gothic church.

SHUBUTA

Shubuta Baptist Church, built in 1894, has simpler vernacular Gothic detailing. Its doors and windows have angular peaks like those at Carrollton Presbyterian Church, the Church of the Good Shepherd at Terry, and St. Joseph Catholic Church in Woodville.

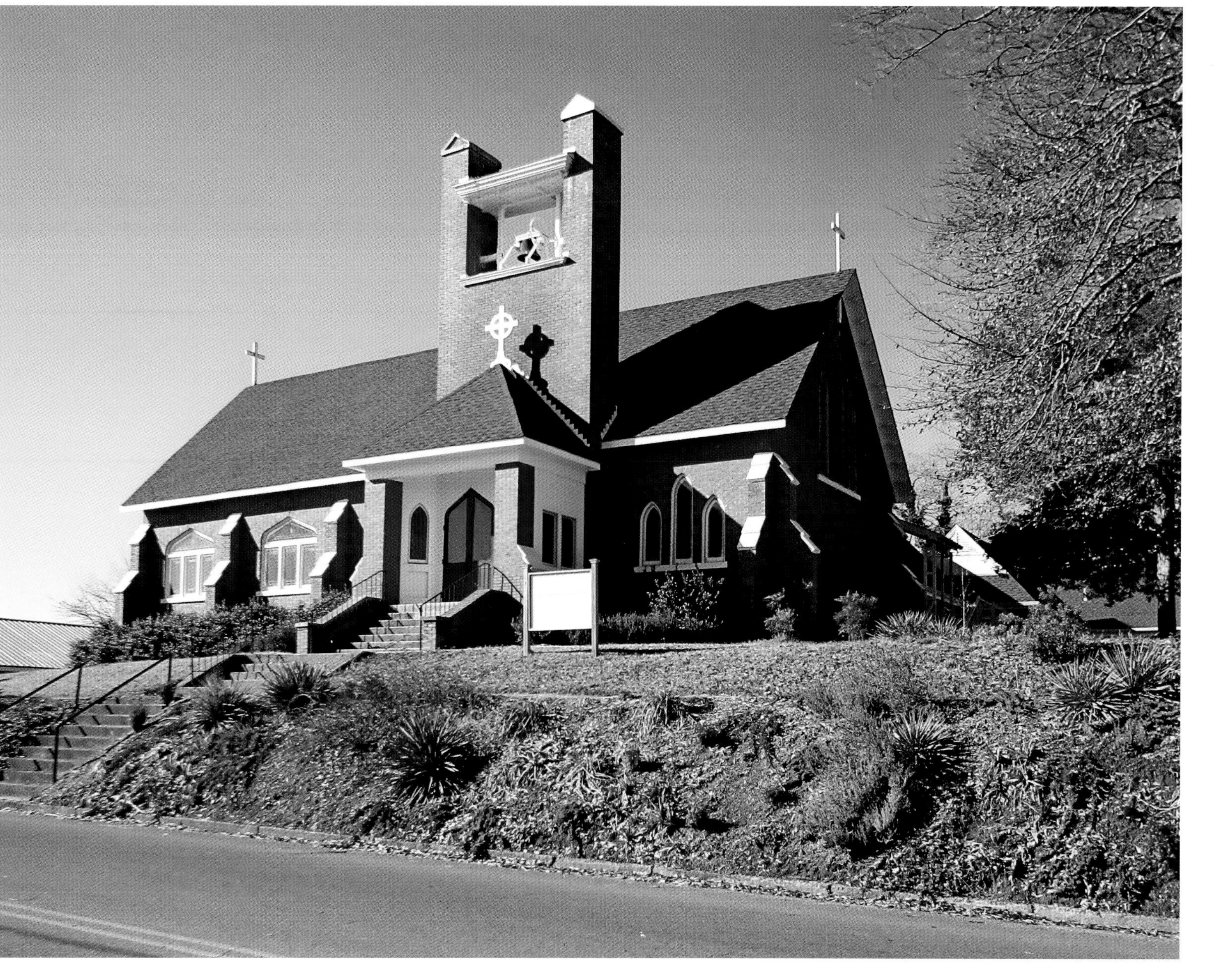

STARKVILLE

The Episcopal *Church of the Resurrection* was built in 1913. The designs of this church and Grace Episcopal Church in Okolona are based on that of St. Columb's Chapel in Jackson, which no longer stands.

STARKVILLE

Starkville has two substantial Neoclassical Revival churches of somewhat similar appearance. Both are brick buildings with projecting, semi-recessed porticoes in the Tuscan order and two tiers of windows on the front façade, but careful examination reveals subtle differences in their design. *First United Methodist Church*, built in 1925, has paired columns at each end of its portico with more widely spaced columns between them.

STARKVILLE

The present sanctuary of *First Presbyterian Church* was built in 1925–26 to replace a Greek Revival church, built in 1855, which had stood on the same site. Like First United Methodist Church, this is a brick Neoclassical Revival building with a Tuscan portico. It is almost identical in appearance to First Presbyterian Church in Covington, Tennessee.

TERRY

The Episcopal *Church of the Good Shepherd* in Hinds County is a vernacular Gothic Revival church built in 1860. The vertical board-and-batten siding is typical of mid-nineteenth-century Carpenter Gothic churches and can also be seen on Grace Episcopal Church in Canton, the Church of Our Savior in Iuka, and Sacred Heart Catholic Church, now at Grand Gulf Military Park near Port Gibson.

TERRY

The windows of the Church of the Good Shepherd are topped with angular peaks instead of curved pointed arches. Similar peaked windows can be seen on several other vernacular Gothic Revival churches.

VAIDEN

Built in 1874, *Shongalo Presbyterian Church* is a rare surviving example of a traditional vernacular building form consisting of two stories, with the upper story serving as a fraternal lodge hall and the lower story serving as a church.

VAIDEN

The transom over the entrance of Shongalo Presbyterian Church and the flanking windows have equilateral pointed arches containing the simplest form of Gothic tracery, a "V" formed by two opposingly curved muntins.

VAIDEN

St. Clement's Episcopal Church is a modest Gothic Revival building constructed in 1876.

VAIDEN

Vaiden United Methodist Church, built in 1871, shows the persistence of vernacular Greek Revival architectural tastes during the years soon after the Civil War.

VICKSBURG

Built between 1839 and 1841, *Christ Church* (Episcopal) was one of the earliest churches in the state to be designed with a consistent Gothic Revival stylistic character.

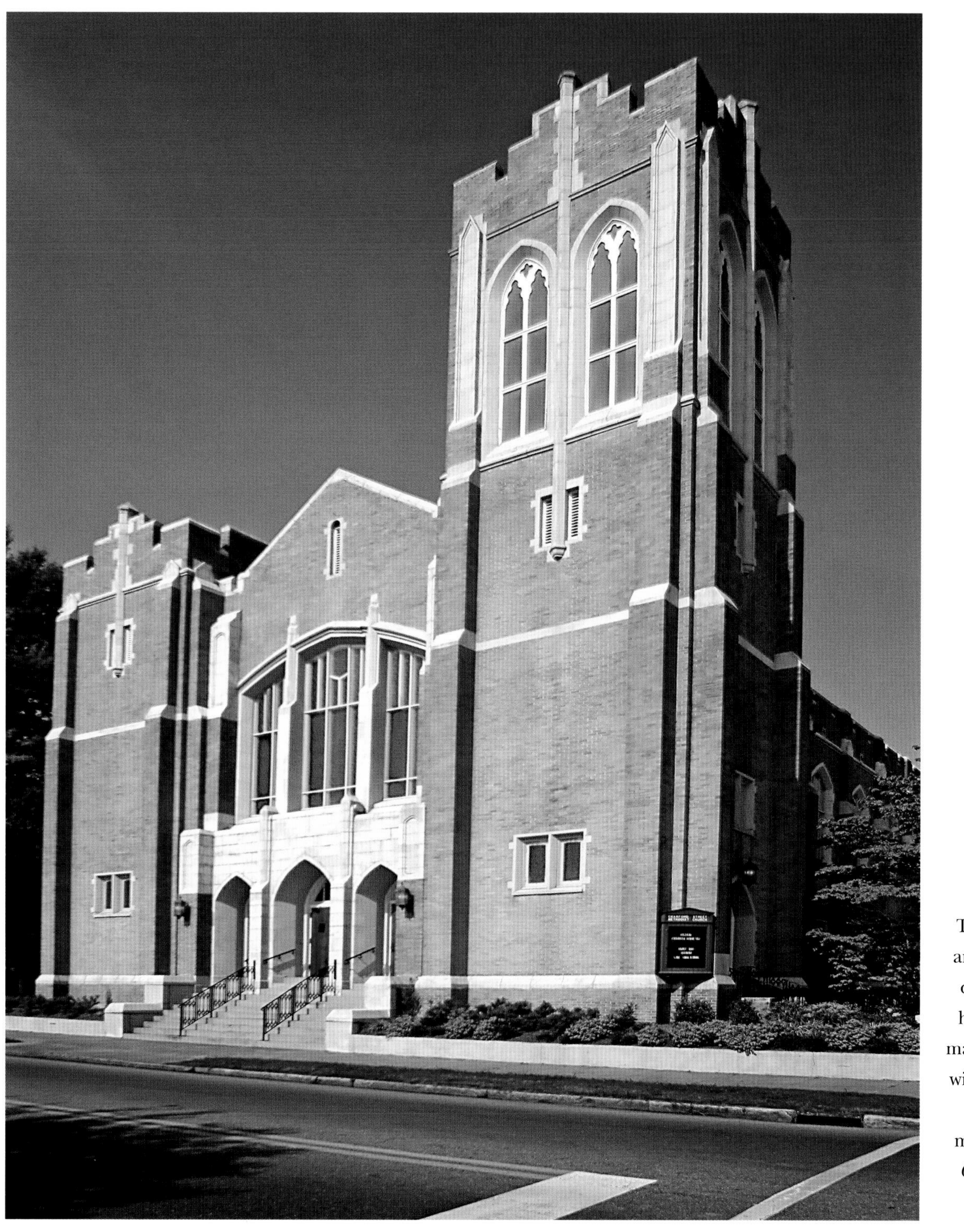

VICKSBURG

The Gothic Revival religious architecture of the 1920s and 1930s typically differed from that of the preceding decades by having a more formal composition, with a highly articulated entrance portal in the center of the main façade, usually surmounted by an elaborate central window, but with fewer other openings, and with flatter, smoother walls and less-pronounced buttresses and moldings. Built in 1925, *Crawford Street United Methodist Church* exemplifies this approach to Gothic design, as does First Presbyterian Church of Greenwood.

VICKSBURG

One of the many churches designed by R. H. Hunt, *First Presbyterian Church*, built from 1906 to 1908, is Mississippi's only example of a church built of stone in the Richardsonian Romanesque style.

VICKSBURG

The *Church of the Holy Trinity* (Episcopal) is the finest example of "High Victorian Romanesque" religious architecture in Mississippi. Begun in 1870 and completed in 1880, it is notable for its fine brickwork, its ornate polychrome patterned slate roof, and its beautiful stained-glass windows.

VICKSBURG

St. Mary's Episcopal Church, built in 1928, has an Italian Romanesque character.

WATER VALLEY

First Christian Church, built about 1905, is an eclectic Romanesque Revival building with a corner entrance tower surmounted by a pyramidal spire.

WESSON

Wesson Presbyterian Church, completed in 1878, is a well-preserved late nineteenth-century Carpenter Gothic church. It has some unusually sophisticated Gothic detailing for a church of wood construction, including the diagonal buttresses at the corners of the center tower.

WESSON

The tower of the Wesson Presbyterian Church is surmounted by a tall octagonal spire.

WINONA

Chattanooga architect R. H. Hunt designed numerous substantial Romanesque Revival auditorium-plan churches throughout the South, including several in Mississippi. One of the most intact is *Moore Memorial United Methodist Church*, built in 1898. This church is very similar in exterior appearance to the old sanctuary of First Baptist Church in Elberton, Georgia, which was also designed by Hunt and was built in 1897.

WINONA

First Presbyterian Church is an elegant small Neoclassical Revival brick church built in 1913. The façade has a tetrastyle portico in the Roman Ionic order.

WINONA

Immanuel Church is an eclectic Gothic Revival church built in 1909–10 for an Episcopal congregation. The building is almost identical to the Church of the Nativity in Greenwood, built in 1902, though the plan is reversed.

WINONA

The tower of Immanuel Church combines Gothic and Classical elements. The arched openings and quatrefoil moldings are Gothic, but the fluted corner pilasters and denticulated cornice are Classical features.

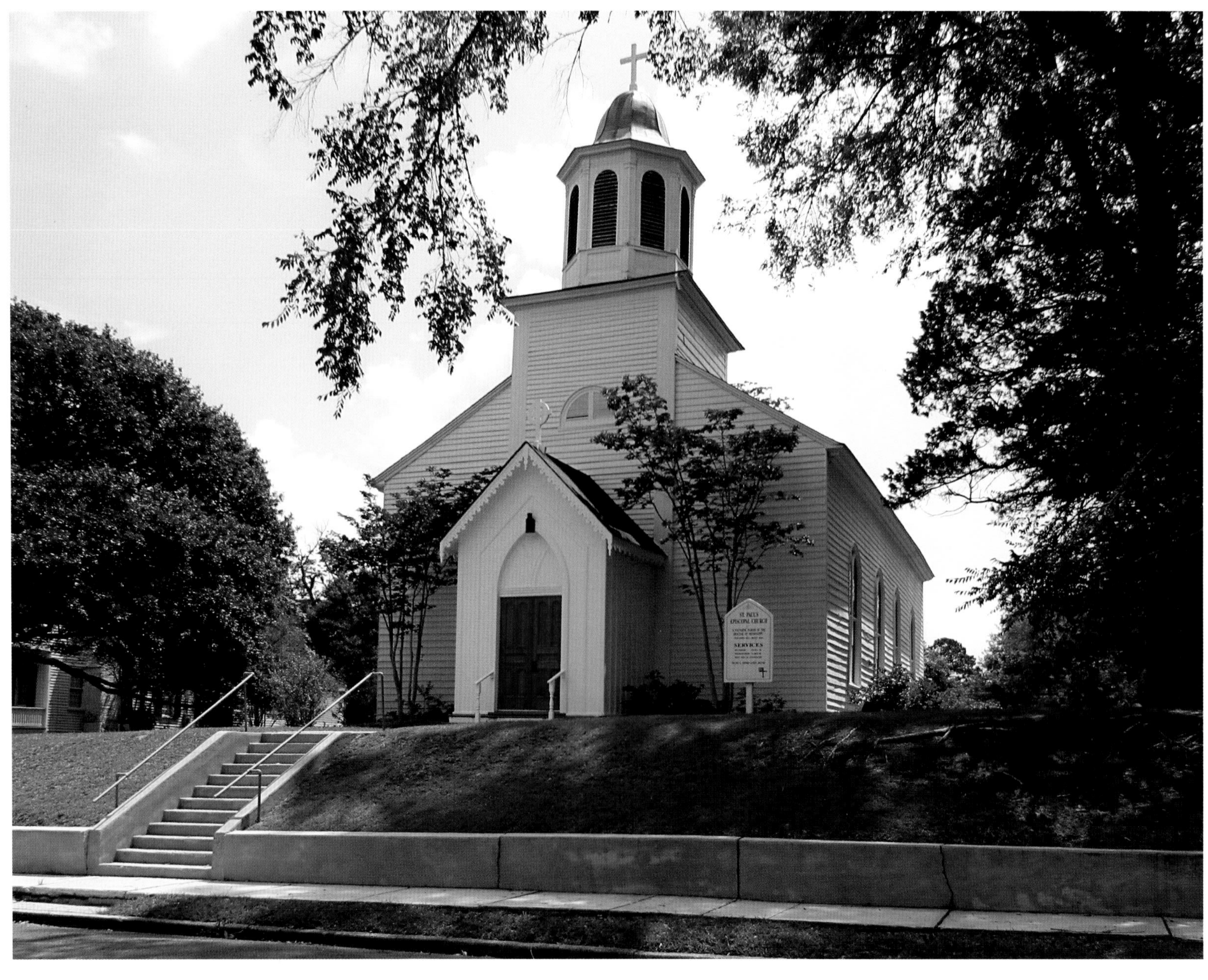

WOODVILLE

Built in 1824, *St. Paul's Episcopal Church* is a Federal-style building with a Gothic Revival entrance vestibule.

WOODVILLE

The projecting entrance vestibule of St. Paul's is trimmed with delicate Gothic Revival vergeboards.

WOODVILLE

A small church of wooden construction with vernacular Gothic detailing, *St. Joseph Catholic Church* was built in 1873.

WOODVILLE

One of three early nineteenth-century churches in Woodville with a Federal-style cupola, *Woodville Baptist Church* is a brick building with twin entrances sheltered by a Tuscan portico.

WOODVILLE

Woodville United Methodist Church was originally built in 1824, though it has had some later alterations.

WOODVILLE

Woodville Presbyterian Church, constructed in 1909, is a vernacular Gothic Revival building with a corner tower.

YAZOO CITY

Although the building has had alterations, *Bethel African Methodist Episcopal Church*, an African American church built in 1891, retains its historic Romanesque Revival tower.

YAZOO CITY

The steeple of Bethel A.M.E. Church is clad in sheet metal panels stamped to resemble shingles.

YAZOO CITY

First United Methodist Church was completed in 1907, replacing an earlier building that was lost in the devastating fire that destroyed much of downtown Yazoo City in 1904. The Gothic Revival building has two towers of unequal height.

YAZOO CITY

The towers of First United Methodist Church are topped with crenellations (also called battlements).

YAZOO CITY

Built from 1905 to 1907, *St. Mary's Catholic Church* is an austere Romanesque Revival building with two identical front corner towers. Typically, where Catholic churches of the nineteenth and early twentieth centuries have two towers, the towers are identical and placed symmetrically at the corners of the front façade, as can also be seen at St. Alphonsus Catholic Church in McComb. In contrast, where Protestant churches have two towers, they are usually not symmetrical.

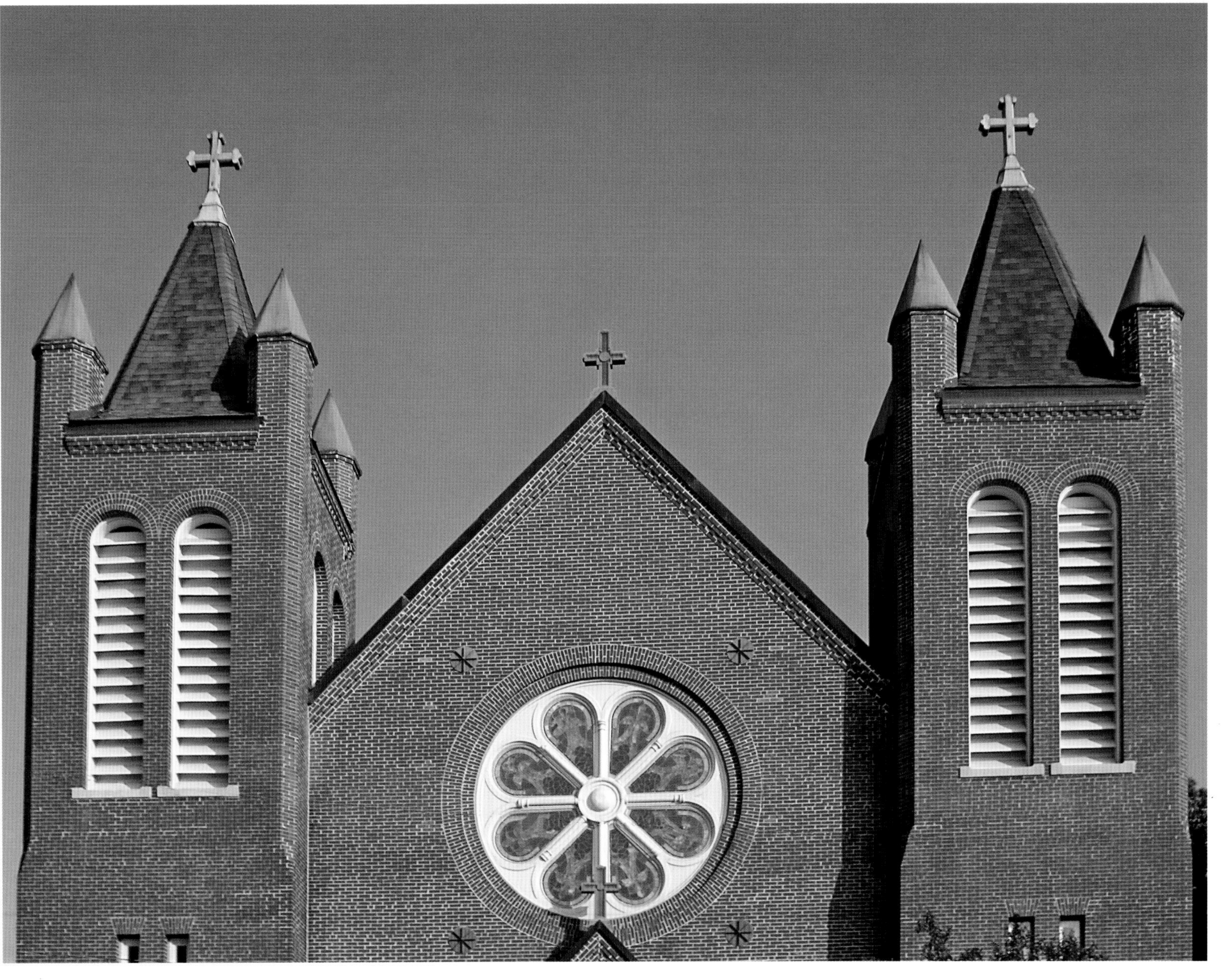

YAZOO CITY

The twin towers of St. Mary's flank a single, large circular stained-glass window located in the upper façade above the entrance portal. A window of this type is called a rose window.

YAZOO CITY

First Presbyterian Church is an auditorium-plan church built in 1905–6. Its unusual diagonally positioned corner tower originally had a tall spire, which was destroyed by a tornado in 1933.

Index of Town Names